Catholic Social Learning

Catholic Social Learning
Educating the Faith That Does Justice

ROGER BERGMAN

FORDHAM UNIVERSITY PRESS
NEW YORK 2011

Library of Congress Cataloging-in-Publication Data

Bergman, Roger (Roger C.)
Catholic social learning : educating the faith that does justice / Roger Bergman.—1st ed.
p. cm.
Includes bibliographical references (p.) and index.
ISBN 978-0-8232-3328-1 (cloth : alk. paper)
ISBN 978-0-8232-3329-8 (pbk. : alk. paper)
ISBN 978-0-8232-3330-4 (ebook)
1. Social justice—Catholic Church—Study and teaching. 2. Christian sociology—Catholic Church—Study and teaching. 3. Catholic Church—Education. I. Title.
BX1795.S62B47 2011
261.8—dc22

2010033992

Printed in the United States of America
13 12 11 5 4 3 2 1
First edition

CONTENTS

PREFACE

Many years ago, I asked the students in an introductory Christian ethics course, "Why are there poor people?" After some moments of uncomfortable silence, one student threw caution to the wind, raised his hand, and volunteered, "To clean up after us?" More recently, one of my students acknowledged in a reflection paper that "living in solidarity with the poor is hard, but I can't imagine not trying." The distance between those two comments, between moral naïveté and committed moral self-identity,[1] is enormous. How is that distance traversed? What sort of bridge can Catholic higher education provide to facilitate the journey?

This book is an attempt to answer that question. As the title *Catholic Social Learning* suggests, it is not sufficient to name the *goal* of the journey as commitment to Catholic social *teaching* (CST). The difference between those two students is not simply that one might have read a social encyclical, and the other probably had not. The difference is not one homework assignment, one courageous homily, one engaging film, or even an entire course on CST. The problem is, in part, to be found within CST itself.

In the approximately 600 pages of the standard collection of documents that represent the canon of CST,[2] only one and one-half pages are devoted explicitly to Catholic social learning or pedagogy. (Those brief comments will be explored in Chapter 1.) This book aims to help correct that gross imbalance. As the articulation of what I have learned from 30 years as a faith-that-does-justice educator, for the past 15 years in a Jesuit university, this is a very personal book, but it is also one that attempts to bring some of the best of current scholarship as well as historical authorities to bear on the topic.

Part I lays the "Foundations" of the book. Chapter 1, "Personal Encounter: The Only Way," includes a faithjustice[3] autobiography and biographical sketches of witnesses more luminary than I. This opening chapter sets the basic theme of the book. How do we move our students from naïveté to solidarity? What makes the crucial difference? In the words of Catholic philosopher of religion Gabriel Marcel, "Through personal encounters. Nothing else ever changes anyone in an important way." It is personal encounter and relationship with the poor and marginalized that stimulates a hunger and thirst for justice and therefore a commitment to Catholic social teaching.

Chapter 2, "Ignatian Pedagogy and the Faith That Does Justice," presents the Pedagogical Circle as the appropriate and necessary extension of this insight about the importance of personal encounter. I trace the evolution of the pedagogical circle from the well-known Pastoral Circle of Holland and Henriot, through the "see-judge-act" methodology of Catholic Social Action, to the long-honed practices of Ignatian pedagogy, to the *phronesis* or practical reasoning of Aristotle. The philosophical and ecclesial pedigree of the Pedagogical Circle demonstrates that it need not be thought of as exclusively the property of Jesuit education but is equally at home in all Catholic educational enterprises.

Chapter 3, "Teaching Justice After MacIntyre: Toward a Catholic Philosophy of Moral Education," puts the Pedagogical Circle into cultural-historical context. The philosopher Alasdair MacIntyre argued that social practices within a community of tradition and moral enquiry are the only context in which genuine virtue can be cultivated because meaningful understandings of virtue must be determinate and demandingly particular. I argue that Catholic social pedagogy must be understood in this perspective, but also that understanding the communitarian roots of Catholic social teaching rebuts MacIntyre's colorful assertion that universal human rights are no more real than witches or unicorns.

Part II, "Applications," offers three chapters that examine particular curricular instantiations (social practices) of the foundational insights of Part I. Chapter 4, "Immersion, Empathy, and Perspective Transformation: *Semestre Dominicano*, 1998," analyzes an example of an intensive form of the Pedagogical Circle, of justice pedagogy. *Semestre Dominicano* offered a small group of undergraduate students a four-month experience of cross-cultural immersion, service among the poor and oppressed, social analysis, theological and normative reflection, and personal discernment. I was accompanying faculty for one such group of 16 students in the spring of 1998. Chapter 4 is my narrative and analysis of their experience, especially of "moral anguish."

But one need not leave the United States or even one's hometown to have similar experiences. Chapter 5, "'We Make the Road by Stumbling': Aristotle, Service-Learning, and Justice," argues for well-integrated service-learning as an effective pedagogy for justice. Students in such programs often report experiencing painful emotions in homeless shelters and other domestic sites where their previously unacknowledged privilege is put in shocking contrast with the hardships faced by the poor. If, as Aristotle contended, we learn virtue by doing virtuous acts, our doing and learning, in a world of stark social disparity, may often require a painful stumbling along the way.

Chapter 6, "Meetings with Remarkable Men and Women: On Teaching Moral Exemplars," also relies heavily on Aristotelian insights. The philosopher's analyses of the "semi-virtue" of shame and of the emulous and noble character of the young provide fascinating starting points for a consideration of a classroom pedagogy focused on the study of such emulable moral exemplars as Dorothy Day and Martin Luther King, Jr. Analyses of the role of saints, of the liminal character of college life, of the "higher self," and of the "developmental imperative" flesh out the central theme.

But, some readers may ask, what does any of this transformative pedagogy properly have to do with the traditional liberal educational mission of the Catholic university? As I demonstrate in Chapter 7, "Education for Justice and the Catholic University: Innovation or Development? An Argument from Tradition," the first installment of Part

III, "Institution and Program," John Henry Cardinal Newman's *The Idea of a University* links the discriminatory oppression of Irish Catholics in his day to their historical exclusion from British higher education. Knowledge for its own sake is knowledge for the sake of the student, especially those historically marginalized, and through them for the world and its justice. Pope John Paul II makes a similar argument in *Ex Corde Ecclesiae*. Chapter 7 also traces Ignatius of Loyola's educational pilgrimage through the best universities of sixteenth-century Europe and the establishment by the newly founded Society of Jesus of the world's first school *system*, making the saint the world's first "superintendent of schools." An exploration of the origins and purposes of those schools reveals that Catholic social learning in higher education is nothing new.

Chapter 8, the final installment of Part III and of the book, titled "Aristotle, Ignatius, and the Painful Path to Solidarity: A Pedagogy for Justice in Catholic Higher Education," has five purposes: (1) I highlight the principle images, arguments, insights, and discoveries of the preceding chapters, in which the legacies of Aristotle and Ignatius play such a prominent role; (2) I bear down more deeply into the question of shame, a perhaps surprising theme in a book on justice education within the academy; (3) I outline how these pedagogical ideas play out and come together in the undergraduate program I have designed and direct; (4) I give some of my students the chance to speak for themselves (the best part of the book!); and (5) I offer 11 theses on young adult vocational development in the context of Catholic higher education. We will look back, we will look deeper, we will look at a model, we will listen, and we will draw some brief conclusions. But first, how do we move from naïveté to solidarity? *Personal encounter: the only way.*

ACKNOWLEDGMENTS

As the articulation of what I have learned from 30 years as a faith-that-does-justice educator, this is a very personal book. Many friends and colleagues who have contributed in one way or another to that three decades of my own learning are named in the book, especially in the "autobiography" in Chapter 1. I hope they realize how grateful I am to them for the distinctive ways each has made a difference in my life, and no doubt in many others.

I especially owe deep gratitude to two friends in faithjustice concerns for many of those 30 years, Fr. Dennis Hamm, S.J., Ph.D. (holder of the Graff Chair in Catholic Theology at Creighton University), and Sr. Mary Ann Zimmer, N.D., Ph.D. (now of Marywood University), as well as to a more recent friend and colleague, Dr. Jennifer Reed-Bouley (College of St. Mary). All three have read and critiqued all or parts of the book as they were drafted, much to its improvement. Another companion in justice education, Dr. Mark Chmiel (St. Louis University), has taught by example during several visits to Creighton and encouraged this project. Dr. Michael Lawler, Professor Emeritus of Theology at Creighton University, graciously agreed to review the completed manuscript and offered invaluable critique, as did Dr. David McMenamin, Director of the PULSE Program at Boston College and a leader in the Commitment to Justice in Jesuit Higher Education.

Cardoner at Creighton, a program for the exploration of vocation, under the leadership of Dr. Kristina DeNeve and funded by Lilly

Endowment, Inc., provided a vFellowship in 2006 that made it possible for me to devote that summer single-mindedly to this project. The previous summer, I spent a wonderful week at Sacred Heart Jesuit Retreat House in Sedalia, Colorado, to discern the wisdom of attempting this book project. I am grateful to Cardoner for support for that retreat as well as for the fellowship.

I was able to commit the summer of 2007 to further work on the book thanks to a research fellowship from Creighton's Graduate School; to its Dean, Dr. Gail Jensen, I offer my thanks. The following summer, I received a grant from the Midwest Consortium on Service-Learning in Higher Education, directed by Dr. Gary Heusel; that grant was facilitated by Dr. Mary Ann Danielson of Creighton's Office for Academic Excellence and Assessment. I am grateful to both of them for supporting the work that led to Chapter 5. Throughout this project, Lynn Schneiderman of Creighton's Reinert Alumni Library has procured many books and articles for me with admirable efficiency through Interlibrary Loan.

I am especially grateful to the editors and officers of Fordham University Press for taking a chance on a first-time book author.

My wife, Dr. Wendy M. Wright, Professor of Theology and holder of the Kenefick Chair in the Humanities at Creighton, would be the first to say that her most significant creations are not her 14 books but our three children, Emily, Elizabeth, and Charles, all young adults with keen consciences for care and justice. Wendy deserves the credit. She also deserves the credit for signing us up for a weekend volunteer trip to Tijuana, Mexico, in 1980. Thus engaged, I put my hand to the plow, and Wendy never looked back. "Those who teach justice shall be like the stars forever" (Daniel 12:3).

The cover photograph of Justice & Peace Studies student Ana Heck, with her friends Biali (left) and Yolanda, residents of Batey 2, a Haitian migrant worker community near the town of Esperanza in the Dominican Republic, is by Rachel Belsha and is used with her permission, for which I am grateful. Ana and Rachel participated in Creighton University's *Encuentro Dominicano* program during the spring semester of 2009.

This book is dedicated to my students in the Justice and Peace Studies Program at Creighton University, past, present, and future. As of May 2011, there will be more than 100 graduates. They cannot possibly know how much they have inspired me and this writing project.

Blessed are those who hunger and thirst
for holiness/righteousness/justice,
for they will be satisfied. (*Matthew* 5:6)

I am a teacher of athletes,

He that by me spreads a wider breast
Than my own proves the width of my own,

He most honors my style who learns
under it to destroy the teacher.

Walt Whitman

PART I FOUNDATIONS

1 Personal Encounter

The Only Way

> Nothing else ever changes anyone in an important way.
>
> *Gabriel Marcel*

The Origins and General Approach of This Book

The inspiration behind *Catholic Social Learning: Educating the Faith That Does Justice* flows from three principal wellsprings: (1) my 30 years as a reflective practitioner of justice education in various faith-related settings; (2) my awareness (for almost as long) that the tradition of Catholic social teaching (hereafter abbreviated as CST) itself has almost nothing to say about Catholic social pedagogy; and (3) my appreciation for and participation (since 1995) in the commitment to justice in Jesuit higher education. I believe that I have learned something from my own experience, that CST has much to learn about pedagogy, and that Ignatian pedagogy is a sure foundation for this enterprise.

A Faith-That-Does-Justice Autobiography

Because my own experience as a "faith-that-does-justice educator" is a principal source for whatever insight this book has to offer, I should say something about my background. The year 1980 was a watershed. I was living in Santa Barbara, California, and active in a poetry writing group that sponsored a series of readings by nationally known poets, among them Carolyn Forché, for whom I was the principal host during her brief stay in Santa Barbara. Only two weeks back from El Salvador, where she had been translating the work of a Salvadoran poet, Claribel Alegría, and doing human rights work for Amnesty International, and where she had been with Archbishop Romero the day before his murder, Forché read the following poem, her own, to an astonished audience[1]:

The Colonel

WHAT YOU HAVE HEARD is true. I was in his house. His wife carried a tray of coffee and sugar. His daughter filed her nails, his son went out for the night. There were daily papers, pet dogs, a pistol on the cushion beside him. The moon swung bare on its black cord over the house. On the television was a cop show. It was in English. Broken bottles were embedded in the walls around the house to scoop the kneecaps from a man's legs or cut his hands to lace. On the windows there were gratings like those in liquor stores. We had dinner, rack of lamb, good wine, a gold bell was on the table for calling the maid. The maid brought green mangoes, salt, a type of bread. I was asked how I enjoyed the country. There was a brief commercial in Spanish. His wife took everything away. There was some talk then of how difficult it had become to govern. The parrot said hello on the terrace. The colonel told it to shut up, and pushed himself from the table. My friend said to me with his eyes: say nothing. The colonel returned with a sack used to bring groceries home. He spilled many human ears on the table. They were like dried peach halves. There is no other way to say this. He took one of them in his hands, shook it in our faces, dropped it into a water glass. It came alive there. I am tired of fooling around he said. As for the rights of anyone, tell your people they can go fuck themselves. He swept the ears to the floor with his arm and held the last of the wine in the air. Something for your poetry, no? he said. Some of the ears on the floor caught this scrap of his voice. Some of the ears on the floor were pressed to the ground.[2]

From conversations with Forché, I learned more about Romero,[3] the new "option for the poor" of the Latin American Catholic Church,[4] and the exciting pastoral and intellectual movement called "liberation theology."[5] The next day, I purchased *A Theology of Liberation* by Gustavo Gutiérrez,[6] devoured it, and moved on to Jon Sobrino's *Christology at the Crossroads*,[7] Juan Luis Segundo's *Liberation of Theology*,[8] and Penny Lernoux's *Cry of the People: United States Involvement in the Rise of Fascism, Torture, and Murder and the Persecution of the Catholic Church in Latin America*.[9] All this led to the discovery of CST.[10] I remember a U.S. missioner to Latin America, probably a Maryknoller, pleading in the *National Catholic Reporter* for North Americans to read *Populorum Progressio*. I did (it's still my favorite encyclical, for reasons that will become apparent), and found my way back to *Gaudium et Spes* and the Second Vatican Council. At the end of that watershed year, four North American church women working with the poor in El Salvador—Sisters Ita Ford, Maura Clark, Dorothy Kazel, and lay missioner Jean Donovan[11]—were raped, assassinated, and buried in a shallow grave. They thus joined their names to the list of martyrs for doing the kind of work I would soon be doing on a much more limited scale and in dramatically safer circumstances.

This was heady stuff for an idealistic young man, a fallen-away Protestant in search of a vocation, a noble purpose. I discovered that I could make a personal relationship with *this* Jesus and with *this* church—or better, that this Jesus and this church were making claims on *me*. I announced to Fr. Virgil Cordano, O.F.M., then pastor of St. Barbara's Parish, "The Old Mission," that I wanted to become Catholic. He directed me toward a sturdy year-and-a-half Rite of Christian Initiation of Adults (RCIA) process under the enlightened guidance of Sr. Anne Dunn, I.H.M. Sponsored by the intrepid Clare Conk (in her post–child-rearing years, she passed the difficult California bar exam on her first attempt without going to law school), I became a Catholic at the Easter Vigil, 1983.

In the meantime, I had managed to find my first vocational home. From 1981–1984 (my early thirties), I was education and media coordinator for Los Niños, a small interfaith nonprofit then headquartered in Santa Barbara, but working on behalf of orphanages and impoverished families in Tijuana, Mexico. I conducted occasional workshops for long-term volunteers at our border facilities; edited a quarterly newsletter for supporters; wrote a ten-session study booklet on world hunger to coincide with the ten days of our primary fund-raiser, the Tortilla Marathon, a 250-mile walk from Santa Barbara to the Mexican border; and compiled a bibliography on women and world hunger. I also spoke to many church groups on hunger issues (with the help especially of research, analysis, and materials by Frances Moore Lappé and Food First/Institute for Food and Development Policy, as well as from Bread for the World), on the nuclear weapons issue (inspired by the 1983 U.S. Catholic bishops pastoral letter, to which I still owe so much), and on U.S. policy in Central America (I co-founded an action group called Peace with Justice in Central America).

During these same years, my wife, Wendy, and I became active in an Amnesty International group, working on behalf of Francisco Laurenzo Pons, a political cartoonist and prisoner of conscience in Uruguay. We signed up because of a story in an Amnesty fund-raising letter about the torture of an anonymous prisoner of conscience—or rather, of his three-year-old daughter, as he watched. Our own daughter Emily was three. Pons, as it turned out, had a three-year-old son who had never seen his father. Perhaps as a result of our work, he was eventually released.

About this same time, a story in *The Catholic Worker* newspaper prompted me to write the following:

Sumpul, River of Infants

Downstream from El Salvador, a Honduran fisherman
pulled in his nets. The day's catch
was five small bodies, bloated, discolored
and stabbed through from front to back—
bayonets, he thought. His legs gave way

as if to a storm. He cried out to Jesus
to take his eyes, his heart, the hands
that pulled in the nets. He who called many
back from the dead and the children to him
out of love, out of pity, must also save these.

The fisherman rose to his work. Tenderly
he untangled flesh from cord and weed
and asked the river to take them back,
upstream with the hope of new life if it could
or else further downstream from El Salvador.[12]

Most importantly during those three formative years with Los Niños, I made a more-or-less monthly trek from Santa Barbara, where both tourists and residents enjoy "another day in paradise," and which is adjacent to Montecito (one of the wealthiest communities in the United States) to the Mexican border. This pilgrimage led me past straw-hatted stoop laborers in the agricultural and horticultural fields of Oxnard but also past wet-suited surfers off Rincon Point; onto the fabled Ventura Highway and through the upscale malls and lifestyle of Thousand Oaks, and into the welter of glitz and greed, freeway congestion, and global diversity that is contemporary Los Angeles. (I once trucked used mattresses from Santa Barbara to a group of Salvadoran refugees in LA, where an estimated one million Salvadorans now live.) I drove past the "Western White House" in San Clemente where Mr. Nixon could watch the sun go down over the sparkling Pacific; through the vast brown fields of Marine Corps Base Camp Pendleton; past the San Onofre nuclear power plant; past immigration checkpoints on the northbound lanes; through the sunny suburban dispositions and prosperity of San Diego—and into Tijuana. Better known as a cheap tourist destination, Tijuana arose before me as the tip of the Third World (or as activists used to say, the "Two-Thirds World"), just a half-day's drive from and through some of the most concentrated and insular abundance and optimism in the world.

From paradise to the garbage dump in one easy slide down the golden coast, once monthly for three years. It raised some questions. How can a line in the sand make such a staggering difference in the life chances for millions of people, depending on which side of that border they were born? And what are my responsibilities, having been born on the lucky side of *la frontera*?

The most pointed and poignant evocation of such questions I have ever encountered comes from my friend Mev Puleo (1963–96),[13] whom I first met when she was a volunteer with Los Niños. She writes, in the introduction to her book, *The Struggle Is One: Visions and Voices of Liberation*,[14] which Robert McAfee Brown in his foreword (p. ix) called the single best introduction for North Americans to the new theology coming from the South:

> Solid and majestic. The stone-carved Jesus towers over the ten million inhabitants of Rio de Janeiro.
>
> Animated and pleading. The eyes of children peer into the windows of our tour bus as it snakes up the hill towards the famous statue of "Christ the Redeemer."
>
> Through the bus windows on the left we see posh hotels, immaculate beaches and expensive tourist shops. The windows on the right tell a different story, of ramshackle homes, children in rags, young and old begging for our coins. The Christ statue comes in and out of view as I gape to the left and to the right.
>
> I was fourteen years old, touring Rio de Janeiro with my family, when I first rode that bus to the statue on the hill. That day, as images of opulence and misery rocked my world, a crisis of conscience took root in me.
>
> The questions planted that day took years to find words: What does it mean to be a "Christian"—a follower of Jesus—in a world of contradictions and conflicts? What does it mean to be on the way to Jesus when I view worlds of poverty from an air-conditioned tour bus? The early Christians were called "followers of the way." What way must we, who live inspired by Jesus of Nazareth, follow today?[15]

The classic query and starting point in Christology, the historical and theological study of Jesus, is Jesus' own question to his disciples, "Who do you say that I *am*?" (Matt 16:15; Mark 8:29; Luke 9:20; emphasis added). Significantly, when the followers of John the Baptist turn the tables and ask Jesus himself who he is, he responds not with titles or creedal formulations but rather with a prophet's *curriculum vitae*, with a list of what he *does*: the lame walk, the blind see, the poor have good news preached to them (Matt 11:2–6; Luke 7:18–23). Mev's questions, and mine, are more in sympathy with the *action* answer of Jesus than with his own *identity* question, however important that is in the history of doctrinal theology.[16]

The particular action question this book asks is, How do we educate ("lead out") the faith that does justice? What pedagogy is needed to make CST no longer the church's alleged "best-kept secret"? It certainly is *not* a secret by virtue of being *kept*. The U.S. bishops' pastoral letters of the 1980s were front-page news even in the secular press, and there are dozens of introductory books and plentiful pastoral resources on CST, not to mention a burgeoning scholarship.[17] Rather, CST has not been *received* or perceived as valuable and important. (You can lead the clergy and the faithful to the encyclicals but. . . .) At this late date, it is either obtuse or disingenuous to suggest otherwise. If what is lacking is definitely not the intellectual content that would *nourish* righteousness or justice or political holiness, how do we stimulate the *hunger and thirst*? How do we encourage the kind of deeply rooted and creative crisis of Christian conscience experienced by Mev Puleo, which seems the only morally and spiritually sane response to the contradictions and conflicts that Mev so eloquently articulates in her words and even more compellingly in her photographs?[18]

Always a highlight of my time along the border in the early '80s was a visit to one of the several orphanages supported by Los Niños:

The Bath

Small brown bodies are lathering up.
Four o'clock, shower-time, at the Orphanage of Glory,
Tijuana. I'm here with green bananas.
A truck hit a stone on the way to market,

but there is no market for dumped bananas.
Now small brown bodies gobble them up
and play ball in the concrete courtyard,
spindly roses drying to the walls.

Pop-ups fall in a lone orange tree.
It is hot. We are tired. We've been playing

all day. "*Acapuche! Acapuche!*" and they grab you
for the piggyback ride you've been coached to give.

We are here with green bananas. Loretta
is sick and sleeps on one of our laps.
Perhaps she has parents who will come for her.
"*Pronto! Pronto!*" Oscar shouts in my ear.

We are lathering up. Small brown bodies,
one skinny white. Where arms can't reach,
we scrub each other. We are slippery with laughter.
The smallest need toweling. Someone, bring us clothes.

And to the Tijuana city garbage dump:

Sacrifice at the Dump

Stink. A corner of the dump is burning.
Smoke from old tires smothers the air
for days, rubber dying hard and slow.
The Tijuana Fire Department, some battered
trucks, a few hundred gallons, doesn't come,
doesn't know, couldn't help if it did. Isn't wanted.
This fire, like others, was set with a purpose,
but not vengeance, not insurance, not even for fun.
People are burning to feed their kids.

It's the steel they're after in the belted radials,
set free from the burden of balding, lopsided
or punctured flesh, and valuable now
the fire's cold, the wire coiled,
at the scrap-metal salvage halfway to town.

The men go home under clear skies
black as miners, proud of their work,
with blackened breath and money enough
for beans for a week, beans all around.[19]

As I hope these poems suggest, I was deeply affected by my direct encounters with the poor of Tijuana, tip of the Two-Thirds World, and by my vicarious encounters with the U.S.–sponsored violence in Central America. Whatever good I have done in these last 30 years as an educator for justice springs from those experiences and the deeply unsettling but formative questions they raised. In one high-flying but blunt philosophical/theological anecdote, Daniel Maguire suggests the gist of what this book has to say about Catholic social learning (hereafter abbreviated as CSL) and pedagogy for the faith that does justice:

> In his youth, [the eminent French philosopher Gabriel] Marcel had great antipathy toward religion. Later religion was to become a major concern in his work. Someone asked him how such a dramatic shift had come to be. His answer was dogmatically existentialist: "*Through personal encounters. Nothing else ever changes anyone in an important way.*"[20]

Pope Paul VI Discovers a Suffering World

One need not be a dogmatic existentialist to believe that personal encounter is the key to perspective transformation and therefore to an effective justice pedagogy. All it takes is simple observation. I mentioned earlier that Pope Paul VI's *Populorum Progressio* (PP, 1967), or *The Development of Peoples*, is my favorite encyclical.[21] Here's why: As John R. Popiden points out in his entry on Paul VI in *The New Dictionary of Catholic Social Thought*, one of the keys to understanding this pope's social thought was "the willingness of Paul VI to undertake foreign travel. As the first world-traveling pope, Paul VI made ten major trips to visit the people of such places as the Holy Land, India, Turkey, Bogota [Colombia], Kampala [Uganda], the Philippines, Australia, Hong Kong, and Singapore."[22] The pope himself refers to these travels in the opening paragraphs of his great letter:

> Before we became pope, two journeys, to Latin America in 1960 and to Africa in 1962, brought us into *direct contact* with the acute problems pressing on continents full of life and hope. Then on becoming father of all we

> made further journeys, to the Holy Land and India, and were able *to see and virtually touch* the very serious difficulties besetting peoples of long-standing civilizations who are at grips with the problem of development. (PP #4; emphasis added)

This direct contact with the people and their problems explains, I believe, the urgency with which the pope addresses the issues raised. That urgency is manifest, for example, when he writes:

> When so many people are hungry, when so many families suffer from destitution, when so many remain steeped in ignorance, when so many schools, hospitals, and homes worthy of the name remain to be built, all public or private squandering of wealth, all expenditure prompted by motives of national or personal ostentation, every exhausting armaments race, becomes an intolerable scandal. We are conscious of our duty to denounce it. Would that those in authority listened to our words before it is too late! (PP #53)

In another early paragraph, the pope observes that "today the peoples in hunger are making a dramatic appeal to the peoples blessed with abundance. The Church shudders at this cry of anguish and calls each one to give a loving response of charity to this brother's cry for help" (PP #3). Eighty-some paragraphs later, after a searching social analysis transmutes that appeal to charity into the demand for "bold transformations, [and] innovations that go deep" (PP #32), for "social justice" (PP #44), in the very last paragraph of the encyclical the pope makes that cry for help his own: "For if the new name for peace is development, who would not wish to labor for it with all his powers? Yes, we ask you, all of you, to heed *our cry of anguish*, in the name of the Lord" (PP #87; emphasis in original). In the encyclical's "Final Appeal," the pope gives to educators the "task to awaken in persons, from their earliest years, a love for the peoples who live in misery" (PP #83). How else to do this except by the same process which the Pope himself came to such a heightened sense of urgency regarding "peoples who live in misery"? What is that way? Ask Mev Puleo, ask Gabriel Marcel, ask the author of this book—ask, I dare say, almost anyone who has made a personal commitment to the hard work of social justice: *Through personal encounters. Nothing else ever changes anyone in an important way.*

After three years with Los Niños, which included an illuminating ten-day seminar in Mexico City with the aptly named GATE (Global Awareness Through Experience), I decided that I needed theological training to buttress my burgeoning sense of vocation to lay social justice ministry. I chose Weston Jesuit School of Theology in Cambridge, Massachusetts, because of its excellent reputation and because I would be able to take courses from Fr. David Hollenbach, S.J., whom I still regard as one of if not the outstanding Catholic social ethicist in the United States. So Wendy and I and daughters Emily (then 6) and Elizabeth (1) moved across country in an old green Toyota station wagon. Before departure, Clare Conk and her husband, George, and other friends at the Old Mission, including especially Fr. Virgil, initiated a fund for lay theological education; as far as I know, I was to be the only recipient. We gathered in a backyard and sang "Here I Am, Lord, Send Me." Feeling nurtured and missioned by the various faith communities of the past three years, I went. Two years later and most of a Masters in Theological Studies completed, during my last six months in Cambridge, Fr. Hollenbach directed me in the Retreat in Daily Life (as described by St. Ignatius in the "19th annotation" to his *Spiritual Exercises*), during which I encountered Jesus as my true and best self, inviolable and forgiving, over against my self-righteous, judgmental, and even violent self—false but real. It was a second powerful sendoff to social ministry.

After Weston (and the birth of son Charles in 1985), I took a job as director of New Covenant Center: Education for Justice and Peace in Omaha, Nebraska, a non-diocesan project of several Catholic religious communities. It looked like what I felt called to do; my elderly mother lived just over three hours away in Manhattan, Kansas, my hometown; and we thought we might be able to afford a house. After four years at New Covenant and a couple of years of adjunct teaching of theological ethics at Creighton University at the invitation of Fr. Richard Hauser, S.J., then chair of the Theology Department, I proposed to Fr. Michael Proterra, S.J., Dean of the College of Arts & Sciences, that a

Catholic and Jesuit school like Creighton ought to have a Justice and Peace Studies program. He agreed, asked me to design such a program, and hired me to be its director. That was in the years 1993–95. We're still in the same comfortable house, and I'm still in the same (nearly) perfect job. Especially after completing a doctorate in education at the University of Nebraska–Lincoln in 2005, it's time to try to organize and articulate what I've learned since 1980.

From Catholic Social Teaching to Catholic Social Learning

Catholic social teaching, in the highly visible example of Paul VI, perhaps the pope most deeply committed to global social justice, harbors the seeds of a Catholic social pedagogy. But at least at the level of magisterial pronouncements, those seeds have fallen on stony ground. In the 14 documents that make up the CST "canon" in O'Brien and Shannon's standard collection, there is almost no mention of how this teaching is to be taught—much less, how it is to be *learned*. Or rather, a default pedagogy is implicit: promulgate the documents, teach the principles, exhort the faithful to put these principles into practice. In fact, one of the pastimes of CST teachers—magisterial, academic, and pastoral—is to propose a list of essential principles, on the undoubtedly correct premise that few of the clergy and even fewer of the faithful will actually read the documents themselves. Scholar Charles Curran is the most elegantly parsimonious, suggesting that the essence of CST can be found in *three* principles.[23] Dr. James Rurak, my CST professor at Weston Jesuit School of Theology in the mid-'80s, argued persuasively that *four* principles captured the foundational dynamic of the CST moral vision. Kenneth Himes, O.F.M., in his excellent introduction to CST,[24] invites reflection on six "fundamental themes." The U.S. bishops promote for pastoral teaching purposes seven basic principles to guide Catholic social action.[25] More expansively, the bishops propose ten principles that constitute "a Catholic framework for economic life."[26] Fr. William Byron, S.J., former president of Catholic University of America and a highly credible and public apologist for CST, similarly offers ten principles that encompass CST[27] (and not just its economic vision, although that has tended to dominate other social justice concerns, especially racism, about which the major documents are virtually silent[28]). Finally, Thomas Massaro, S.J., proposes "nine key themes" of CST in his handy textbook.[29]

The default pedagogy of CST is top-down in two ways. First, it is initiated by popes and bishops, and by the time it filters down to the faithful (if it does), it is reduced to principles from which, second, we are supposed to deduce action strategies. I do not exempt myself from blame for practicing this faulty default pedagogy. Despite my aversion to what Paulo Freire famously described as "banking education"—in which the teacher, who possesses knowledge as if from on high, deposits it in the empty accounts (minds) of his passively receptive students[30]—I have given hundreds of talks in parishes and other venues where I have been the one doing the filtering and deducing and exhorting. It has never made sense to turn down such invitations (and I do try to be more dialogical than my self-caricature suggests), but I am not aware that any of those hundreds of talks have made any significant difference to anyone, at least not directly, and certainly not to the poor, however indirectly. As rhetorically persuasive, informed, hopeful, and engaging as I try to be, I have witnessed no transformation of perspective, no deep clarification of moral vision, no galvanizing of the will that would catapult even an already sympathetic Catholic into action that by definition often goes against the culture. Still, I have never turned down an invitation to try it one more time. But there must be a better way.

And there is. CST, as I said earlier, is not completely clueless. That remarkable statement from the 1971 Rome Synod of Bishops, *Justitia in Mundo*, or *Justice in the World* (JW), is the sole CST document to address Catholic social pedagogy, in a brief but pregnant section titled "Educating to Justice."[31]

"Educating to Justice" in *Justice in the World*

In the approximately 600 pages of the Catholic social teaching texts in O'Brien and Shannon, we have to settle for a page and a half on

Catholic social pedagogy (pages 296–97; all subsequent quotations are from these pages). But those 11 short paragraphs are packed and, indeed, provide the essential elements of an authentic and effective CSL, one that Paul VI surely could have affirmed from his own experience.

The section begins by encouraging cultural analysis: an example, however cursory, of the "scrutinizing the signs of the times and interpreting them in the light of the gospel" called for by Vatican II in *Gaudium et Spes* (#4). We face three major cultural obstacles (I presume they are still with us) to an evangelical witness for justice: narrow individualism, materialism and consumerism, and schooling and mass media that are dysformative of the human person as envisioned by Christian anthropology:

> The obstacles to the progress which we wish for ourselves and for mankind are obvious. The method of education very frequently still in use today encourages narrow individualism. Part of the human family lives immersed in a mentality which exalts possessions. The school and communications media, which are often obstructed by the established order, allow the formation only of the man desired by that order, that is to say, man in its image, not a new man but a copy of man as he is.[32]

But if education is part of the problem, it is also part of the solution. Persons as they are, deformed and manipulated by the cultural forces of excessive individualism and acquisitiveness, are not a lost cause. But the necessary pedagogy must be holistic and *trans*formative:

> But education demands a renewal of heart, a renewal based on the recognition of sin in its individual and social manifestations. It will also inculcate a truly and entirely human way of life in justice, love, and simplicity. It will likewise awaken a critical sense, which will lead us to reflect on the society in which we live and on its values; it will make men ready to renounce these values when they cease to promote justice for all men.

One wonders whether some of the bishops or their *periti* (expert advisors) might have been aware of Paulo Freire's *Pedagogy of the Oppressed*, which theorizes about his pioneering work in literacy education among the poor and marginalized of his native Brazil,[33] when one reads what could almost be a characterization of Freire's *conscientização* (the Portuguese is usually translated as "conscientization," meaning both social consciousness-raising and conscience-formation).[34] The bishops write:

> In the developing countries, the principal aim of this education for justice consists in an attempt to awaken consciences to a knowledge of the concrete situation and in a call to secure a total improvement; by these means the transformation of the world has already begun. . . . It will . . . enable them to take in hand their own destinies and bring about communities which are truly human.

Compare that with the way that Freire himself describes pedagogy of the oppressed:

> In problem-posing education, people develop their power to perceive critically *the way they exist* in the world *with which* and *in which* they find themselves; they come to see the world not as a static reality, but as a reality in process, in transformation. . . . The world—no longer something to be described with deceptive words—becomes the object of that transforming action by men and women which results in their humanization. (*Pedagogy*, pages 64, 67; emphasis in original)

But the transformative education that we are concerned with in this book is not first of all *of* the poor, however much it is *on behalf* of the poor. The bishops seem to take this same perspective when they advise that education for justice is "a practical education: it comes through action, participation, and *vital contact* with the reality of injustice" (emphasis added). Freire's illiterate and oppressed peasants do not need to seek out contact with injustice; that is their reality. Rather, they need to "awaken," to recognize their reality for what it is and also that it does not have to be that way.

But for those of us whose reality is defined by individualism, acquisitiveness, and the manipulation of the mass media—by big-box retail warehouses and not by the city dump, for those of us on the lucky side of the border—educating to justice must be very intentional about discovering other realities, the realities those peasants and the rest of the Two-Thirds World are submerged in every day. It's about discovering a greater truth. As Dan Hartnett, S.J. argues, "by situating ourselves alongside the poor, and by appreciating the hermeneutical lens that this provides, we achieve a 'double contact' with reality that offers a healthy corrective to the limitations of our 'natural' involvement in the world. It seems to me that this should mean greater, not less, objectivity."[35] Educating to justice, then, is all about crossing borders, and not just lines in the sand. The distance from my life to that of the Tijuana father scavenging in the city dump is more than the 250 miles I drove once per month for three years from Santa Barbara. It's a universe, and the "space travel" required to get there is as demanding of courage and intelligence as flying to the moon—and a good deal more Gospel-driven.

So *Justice in the World* gives us an insightful glimpse of what we're up against and the process by which we overcome it, but what's in the syllabus of that pedagogy?

> The content of this education necessarily involves respect for the person and for his dignity. Since it is world justice which is in question here, the unity of the human family within which, according to God's plan, a human being is born must first of all be seriously affirmed. Christians find a sign of this solidarity in the fact that all human beings are destined to become in Christ sharers in the divine nature. (JW, p. 296)

Allow me to emphasize that it is only *after* cultural or social analysis and only *after* outlining a pedagogy that the bishops enunciate principles. The foregoing sentences are an extremely parsimonious description of the essence of CST: human dignity and solidarity with God as our source and destiny. But what texts might we study?

> The basic principles whereby the influence of the Gospel has made itself felt in contemporary social life are to be found in the body of teaching set

> out in a gradual and timely way from the encyclical *Rerum Novarum* [1891] to the letter *Octogesima Adveniens* [earlier in 1971]. (JW, p. 296)

The backbone of the formal curriculum, of course, is Catholic social teaching, the "documentary heritage," which now also includes the three social encyclicals of Pope John II; Pope Benedict XVI's *Caritas in Veritate* (Charity in Truth); and, for U.S. Catholics, the two major pastoral letters, *The Challenge of Peace* (1983) and *Economic Justice for All* (1986), and other documents such as the quadrennial *Faithful Citizenship*, of the U.S. bishops. And each of those documents, it should be pointed out, does more than enunciate principles and exhort the faithful to live them. They also read the signs of the times (do social analysis), and make recommendations for public policy, "in conformity with circumstances of place and time." That suggests that not only social ethics but also the social sciences are essential ingredients in the full scope of Catholic social leaning. More on that in Chapter 8.

Finally, *Justice in the World* points out that

> The liturgy, . . . which is the heart of the Church's life, can greatly serve education for justice. For it is a thanksgiving to the Father in Christ, which through its communitarian form places before our eyes the bonds of our brotherhood and again and again reminds us of the Church's mission. The liturgy of the word, catechesis, and the celebration of the sacraments have the power to help us to discover the teaching of the prophets, the Lord, and the apostles on the subject of justice. (JW, p. 297)

The Church's public prayer life, when done liturgically and not just routinely, forms the justice-oriented and communitarian Christian just as educational systems and mass media, if captive to an individualistic and acquisitive culture, deform the human person. "The Eucharist forms the community and places it at the service of men." Or at least it should. But not if it, too, is captive, however subtly, to the surrounding culture, not perhaps by acquisitiveness so much as by an excessively privatized spirituality and a fear of the political and prophetic. But that is a story for another book (and by another author).[36]

What this book proposes, then, is not a departure from what can already be gleaned from CST. Rather, it offers a substantial development of what we can learn from reflection on our own experience, the experience of church leaders such as Pope Paul VI, of lay activists such as Mev Puleo, of my own students at Creighton University (see Chapters 4 and 6), of other university students (see Chapter 5), and of the few words that the tradition itself has to say about a pedagogy that would render CST a well-respected resource. A look at Ignatian pedagogy can help with that development.

2 Ignatian Pedagogy and the Faith That Does Justice

When the heart is touched by direct experience, the mind may be challenged to change.

Fr. Peter-Hans Kolvenbach, S.J.

The Society of Jesus (the Jesuits), the first teaching order in the Church,[1] is known for producing both master teachers and, in the second half of the sixteenth century, the world's first school system, "one of the most successful . . . the Western world has ever seen."[2] Although Ignatius of Loyola had no intention of becoming, in effect, a superintendent of schools when he founded the order in 1540, by the time of his death in 1556, he was overseeing 35 schools still in operation of the 40 he had approved; by the end of the century, when the famous *Ratio Studiorum* (*Plan of Studies* for Jesuit schools) was published, some 245 schools for boys and young men had been founded (p. 224; see note 2). That number had increased to 845 in Europe, the Americas, Asia, and Africa by 1773 when the Society was suppressed. When Pope Pius VII restored the Society in 1814, he wrote that he did so "'so that the Catholic Church could have, once again, the benefit of their [the Jesuits'] educational experience.'"[3] At the turn of the millennium, some 2,000 schools for both boys and girls, men and women, were operating under Jesuit auspices in 56 countries worldwide, involving 10,000 Jesuits, nearly 100,000 lay collaborators, and more than 1.5 million students (p. 230).

From Fe y Alegría primary schools for the poor in Latin America, to the "Nativity" model middle schools and the new Cristo Rey high schools for the disadvantaged in the United States, to college preparatory high schools and colleges and universities throughout the Americas, the Jesuits are a formidable force in education.[4] Especially since its 32nd General Congregation in 1975, when the Society formally and famously, in Decree 4 of its proceedings, named its mission as "the service of faith, of which the promotion of justice is an absolute requirement," Jesuit education has become a formidable force for education *for justice*.[5] That this is true for Jesuit higher education in the United States is demonstrated in the following section.

"The Commitment to Justice in Jesuit Higher Education"

In early 1999, to prepare for the twenty-fifth anniversary of that momentous decision, the presidents of Boston College, University of Detroit Mercy, and Santa Clara University called upon all 28 Jesuit colleges and universities in the United States to participate in local, regional, and national conversations on what had been done and learned in that quarter of a century of "The Commitment to Justice in Jesuit Higher Education."[6] Each school prepared a self-study for presentation at one of three conferences held later that year at the campuses of the initiating presidents. One year later, in October 2000, all 28 schools sent delegations to a national conference hosted by Santa Clara University on the occasion of its 150th anniversary. Follow-up meetings have been held at Loyola University Chicago in 2002, at John Carroll University in Cleveland in 2005, and at Fairfield University in 2009. I have been honored to be the chair of the Creighton delegations to all the conferences we've attended, and therefore also the editor/author of "Education for Justice at Creighton University Since 1975: A Self-Study."[7]

Undoubtedly, the highlight of all these proceedings was the keynote address on October 6, 2000, at Santa Clara by the Rev. Peter-Hans Kolvenbach, S.J., Superior General of the Society of Jesus. Like *Justice in the World*, the document produced by the 1971 Synod of Bishops in Rome, it gives a tantalizing glimpse of a pedagogy adequate to the demands of teaching justice, of Catholic social learning. But before examining that address, we should review its principal recent antecedents.[8]

Fr. Pedro Arrupe, S.J., and "Men and Women for Others" (1973)

Fr. Pedro Arrupe, S.J., like Ignatius of Loyola a Basque, is often referred to as the "second founder" of the Society of Jesus.[9] As his successor Fr. Kolvenbach writes, "as the Jesuit General from 1965 to 1983, Father Arrupe led his brother Jesuits through a challenging period of renewal called for by the Second Vatican Council."[10] Kevin Burke, S.J., expands on this by pointing out that "Arrupe's personal concern for the poor and his visionary reading of the church's social gospel fed his concern to renew the vitality of Christian discipleship around the intrinsic connection between faith and justice. This became the defining mark of his years as the General of the Society of Jesus."[11] This commitment to the poor can be traced at least in part to two *personal encounters* he had as a young medical student in Madrid in the 1920s.

As reported by Ronald Modras,[12] Pedro had been raised in a comfortable if not wealthy Basque family and had had no exposure to destitution. But as a representative of the Society of St. Vincent de Paul, Pedro was sent to an impoverished area of the city. At four in the afternoon, he encountered a young boy eating a roll. He asked whether he was enjoying his afternoon snack. The boy replied, "No. . . . I'm having my breakfast." Further conversation revealed that it was also his lunch and his dinner, as was usual. On another occasion, Pedro and a friend were sent to visit a poor widow in a slum neighborhood. As it turned out, the widow shared a run-down apartment with another widow and six children between them. All eight slept in one bed. During the day, one mother went out to try to earn some money while the other looked after *los niños* (the children). None of the children had winter clothes. Pedro and his friend "walked home in silence." Thirty years later, those two encounters with the poor remained etched on Fr. Arrupe's memory. In the meantime, he had become, like his contemporary, Paul VI, a globetrotter. "The way other world travelers visit museums and tourist sites, Arrupe visited barrios, ghettos, and slums. But he never seemed to forget—even to the point of remembering the smile that froze on his face—encountering a child's hunger for the first time."

Elected Superior General of the Society of Jesus in 1965, Fr. Arrupe not only attended the 1968 Conference of Latin American Bishops (the "Medellin Conference"; Medellin, Colombia) but also encouraged its implementation.[13] His lengthy commentary on *Justice in the World* was published by the Pontifical Commission "Justice and Peace" and includes observations on conscientization and solidarity inspired at least in part by Paulo Freire, to whom he explicitly refers. "Real conscientization (consciousness-raising)," Arrupe wrote, "is a critical insertion in historical reality. That obliges one to accept the role of a subject who makes the world—or better, remakes it. . . . [C]onscientization necessarily includes the combination of our reflection on the world and our action on it. . . . The dialectical unity 'action-reflection' will always be our most distinctive mode of being, our only effective way of changing the world."[14] Arrupe makes explicit the theological underpinning that is usually only implicit in Freire; I quote him at length, as this passage sums up so much of the vision that shapes this book:

> [T]he external reality that we change then changes us in our very depths, and that very change makes us become "agents for change." This interaction is a manifestation and an effect of the intimate action of the Holy Spirit, who integrates, simultaneously and harmonically, the progress of a pilgrim humanity toward its true homeland and my growth in divine life that the Spirit communicates to me. . . . A genuine insertion thus requires a change of personal attitude, the giving up, under many aspects, of our manner of being, thinking, and acting, so we can understand and come closer to the new realities that we want to evangelize. . . . This insertion or "incarnation" means solidarity with those who suffer, even to being identified with their lives. Here we find the most profound meaning of the poverty of the poor Christ, whom we want to imitate and follow. That phrase of the [Spiritual] Exercises [of St. Ignatius] that describes our contemplation—"as if I were actually present"—takes on a vivid meaning that reflects the Gospel words: "What you did to the least of my brothers and sisters, you did to me" (Matt 25:40). . . . It is the apparition of Christ among the poor, his real presence among them.[15]

Given this gospel mandate as refracted through Ignatian spirituality and as affirmed in *Justice in the World*, is it any wonder that Fr. Arrupe would make the link to the primary ministry of the Society, that of education? He did so in "a controversial and widely discussed address to the alumni of Jesuit high schools [in Valencia, Spain, on July 31, the Feast of St. Ignatius, 1973], the title of which was subsequently adopted as the unofficial motto of many Jesuit institutions: 'Men and Women for Others.'" The most frequently quoted lines are these:

> Today our prime educational objective must be to form men-and-women-for-others; men and women who will live not for themselves but for God and his Christ—for the God-human who lived and died for all the world; men and women who cannot even conceive of love of God which does not include love for the least of their neighbors; men and women completely convinced that love of God which does not issue in justice for others is a farce.[16]

Referring to the Second Vatican Council (1962–65), *Populorum Progressio* (1967), the documents of the regional bishops' synods in Latin America (1968), Africa (1969), and Asia (1970), to *Octogesima Adveniens* (1971) and especially to *Justice in the World* (1971), Arrupe notes that such statements "are the resonance of an imperious call of the living God asking his church and all persons of good will to adopt certain attitudes and undertake certain types of action which will enable them effectively to come to the aid of humankind oppressed and in agony."[17] The Society's mission is a direct response: "Men-and-women-for-others: the paramount objective of Jesuit education—basic, advanced, and continuing—must now be to form such men and women. For if there is any substance in our reflections, then this is the prolongation into the modern world of our humanist tradition as derived from the Spiritual Exercises of St. Ignatius."[18] Education for justice is not an add-on nor an option: It is at the heart of Ignatian pedagogy. Nowhere has that educational method for the contemporary world been more comprehensively and authoritatively explicated than in two documents of the last two decades of the twentieth century, to which we now turn.

"The Characteristics of Jesuit Education" (1986)

In 1980, in response to the concerns of Jesuit high school educators from around the world, Fr. Arrupe established the International Commission on the Apostolate of Jesuit Education (ICAJE) to produce a "contemporary identity statement" not to replace but to update the famous *Ratio Studiorum* of 1599, the guiding document for Jesuit education in its early decades and even centuries. As reported by Vincent J. Duminuco, S.J., one of the founding members, the "Commission, with one representative from each continent, worked for over four years through six drafts in moving toward its goal" (p. 151). In 1986, Fr. Kolvenbach, by then Arrupe's successor, made the document his own, sending it to all of the Jesuit provincials. *The Characteristics of Jesuit Education* has been translated into 13 languages and is recommended by Fr. Kolvenbach as a model not just for high schools but also for colleges and universities affiliated with the Society of Jesus (pp. 152–53). This book is a partial response to that appeal.

Characteristics is divided into nine sections, 28 subsections, and introductory and concluding materials plus a three-part appendix. Section 5 is devoted to the Ignatian axiom, "Love is shown in deeds." A footnote points out that "the fundamental basis for the connection between justice and faith has to be seen in the inseparable connection with the new commandment of love. . . . [since] justice is the form which love ought to take in an unjust world" (p. 190). The four subsections address (5.1) "Active life commitment," (5.2) "Education in the service of the faith that does justice," (5.3) "Men and women for others" [quoting the famous paragraph from Fr. Arrupe's 1973 Valencia address], and (5.4) "A particular concern for the poor." Jesuit education for justice has three dimensions:

> 1. Justice issues are treated in the curriculum. . . . which includes a *critical analysis of society* adapted to the age level of the students . . . [as well as]

> the outlines of a solution that is in line with Christian principles. The reference points are the Word of God, church teaching, and human science. . . . 2. The *policies and programs* of a Jesuit school *give concrete witness to the faith that does justice*; they give a counter-witness to the values of a consumer society. . . . 3. "There is no genuine conversion to justice unless there are *works of justice*. . . . [including] opportunities in Jesuit education for actual contact with the world of injustice. . . . [so that the] analysis of society within the curriculum . . . becomes reflection based on actual contact with the structural dimensions of injustice. (pp. 191–92; emphasis in original)

In other words, *Characteristics* recommends something very like the pedagogy sketched in *Justice in the World*: actual contact with injustice, social analysis, and theological reflection—and does so in the context of vocational discernment, "the formation of men and women who will put their beliefs and attitudes into practice throughout their lives" (p. 189).

In what seems a direct response to Paul VI's appeal to educators in *Populorum Progressio* (PP #83), the document urges Jesuit schools to provide students "with *opportunities for contact with the poor and for service to them* . . . to enable these students to learn to love all as brothers and sisters in the human community, and also in order to come to better understanding of the causes of poverty" (p. 195; emphasis in original). And, as a matter of institutional witness (practicing what we preach), in what surely is one of Ignatius' strongest challenges to contemporary U.S. Jesuit higher education especially, the document reminds us that the Society's founder "accepted schools only when they were completely endowed so that education could be available to everyone . . . [and] insisted that special facilities for housing the poor be a part of every school foundation that he approved and that teachers give special attention to the needs of poor students" (p. 194). Indeed, "the poor form the context of Jesuit education: 'Our educational planning needs to be made in function of the poor, from the perspective of the poor'" (p. 195; quoting Gabriel Codina, S.J.). The ideal of Jesuit education, from the time of the earliest schools, has been of the poor themselves and of the nonpoor on behalf of the poor.[19] In other words, "the faith that does justice" may be a linguistic innovation, but in Catholic education, the idea and practice goes back to Ignatius himself. (More on this in Chapter 7.)

"Ignatian Pedagogy" (1993)

But as welcomed and influential as *The Characteristics of Jesuit Education* has been, it was also found to be lacking in practical guidance. In response, the ICAJE produced in 1993, after more than three years of work and seven drafts, a second document, *Ignatian Pedagogical Paradigm*, or *Ignatian Pedagogy*, for short. I reproduce in Figure 2.1 that paradigm in diagram form (Duminuco, *Jesuit Ratio Studiorum*, p. 249).

I quote the description of this paradigm in full:

> Starting with EXPERIENCE, the teacher creates the conditions whereby students gather and recollect the material of their own experience in order to distill what they understand already in terms of facts, feelings, values,

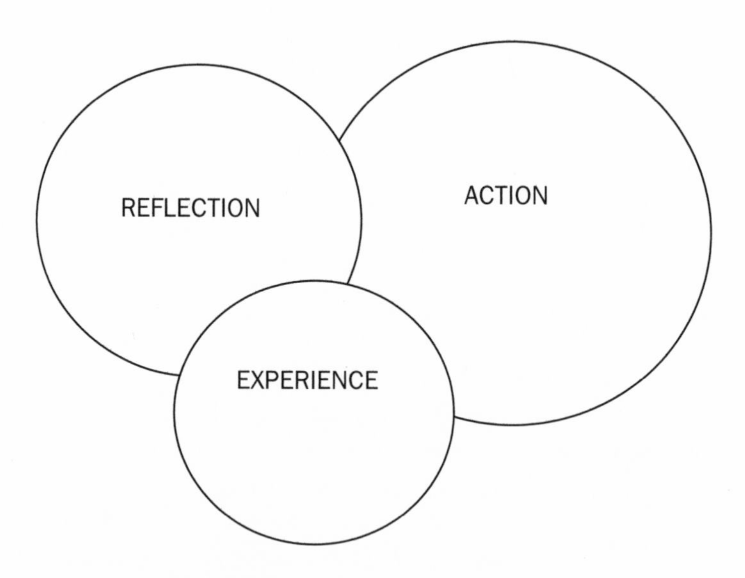

Figure 2.1. Ignatian Paradigm

> insights and intuitions they bring to the subject matter at hand. Later the teacher guides the students in assimilating new information and further experience so that their knowledge will grow in completeness and truth. The teacher lays the foundations for learning how to learn by engaging students in skills and techniques of REFLECTION. Here memory, understanding, imagination and feelings are used to grasp the essential meaning and value of what is being studied, to discover its relationship to other facets of human knowledge and activity, and to appreciate its implications in the continuing search for truth. Reflection should be a formative and liberating process that so shapes the consciousness of students—their habitual attitudes, values and beliefs as well as ways of thinking—that they are impelled to move beyond knowing to ACTION. It is then the role of the teacher to see that the opportunities are provided that will challenge the imagination and exercise the will of the students to choose the best possible course of action to flow from and follow up on what they have learned. What they do as a result under the teacher's direction, while it may not immediately transform the world into a global community of justice, peace and love, should at least be an educational step in that direction and towards that goal even if it merely leads to new experiences, further reflections and consequent actions within the subject area under consideration. The continual interplay, then, of EXPERIENCE, REFLECTION and ACTION in the teaching-learning dynamic of the classroom lies at the heart of an Ignatian pedagogy (pp. 247–48).[20]

The document is at pains to point out that this paradigm is inspired by the human-divine dynamic of the Spiritual Exercises, with the student, teacher, and truth in analogous roles and relationships to the retreatant, director, and God, respectively. And just as the Exercises seek to transform the retreatant's relationship with God, thus

> [E]ducation in Jesuit schools seeks to transform how youth look at themselves and other human beings, at social systems and societal structures, at the global community of humankind and the whole of natural creation. If truly successful, Jesuit education results ultimately in a *radical transformation* [emphasis added] not only of the way in which people habitually think and act, but of the very way in which they live in the world, men and women of competence, conscience and compassion, seeking the *greater*

> *good* [the famous Jesuit "magis"] in terms of what can be done out of a faith commitment with justice to enhance the quality of peoples' lives, particularly among God's poor, oppressed and neglected. (p. 243)

It is a magnificent vision and noble commitment, responding as it does to an educational context that could hardly be any more imperative. "The root issue is this," according to *Ignatian Pedagogy*, in terms that echo Paul VI's "cry of anguish" and are only slightly dated:

> What does faith in God mean in the face of Bosnia and Sudan, Guatemala and Haiti, Auschwitz and Hiroshima, the teeming streets of Calcutta and the broken bodies of Tiananmen Square? What is Christian humanism in the face of starving millions of men, women and children in Africa? What is Christian humanism as we view millions of people uprooted from their own countries by persecution and terror, and forced to seek a new life in foreign lands? What is Christian humanism when we see the homeless that roam our cities and the growing underclass who are reduced to permanent hopelessness. What is humanistic education in this context? (p. 277)

It is in the same context and on behalf of the same basic pedagogy that Fr. Kolvenbach addressed the conference on "The Commitment to Justice in Jesuit Higher Education" at Santa Clara in 2000, in this author's grateful hearing.

"The Service of Faith and the Promotion of Justice in American Jesuit Higher Education"

Fr. Kolvenbach took as his title and theme "The Service of Faith and the Promotion of Justice in American Jesuit Higher Education."[21] After an analysis of "the Jesuit commitment to faith and justice" since 1975 and after a typically Ignatian "'composition' of our time and place" (the Silicon Valley, when advanced market economies were booming but half the world's population still was mired in poverty), Fr. Kolvenbach devoted a section of his address to the question which concerns this book, "Formation and Learning" in the context of faith and justice in higher education. As with *Justice in the World*, we get just a handful of paragraphs, but they take us closer to the pedagogy we seek to develop.

Any coherent educational program must have an end in view and means by which to reach it. Fr. Kolvenbach defines the end of Jesuit higher education not primarily as the "'worldly success' based on marketable skills" of its graduates but rather "in who our students become." For 450 years, that "who" has been defined as "'the whole person,'" which includes not only the intellectual and professional, but also the psychological, moral, and spiritual. But what that means for us is different from what it meant in previous periods of human history. If our students today are to be whole persons tomorrow, they "must have a well-educated solidarity." Therefore, "we must raise our Jesuit educational standard to educate the whole person of solidarity for the real world."[22] But what does that solidarity look like?

Pope John Paul II has described solidarity as "undoubtedly a Christian virtue," by which he means "not a feeling of vague compassion or shallow distress at the misfortunes of so many people, both near and far. On the contrary, it is a *firm and persevering determination* to commit oneself to the common good."[23] For Fr. Kolvenbach, solidarity means letting "the gritty reality of the world" into our lives. Our students should "learn to feel it, think about it critically, respond to its suffering, and engage it constructively. They should learn to perceive, think, judge, choose, and act for the rights of others, especially the disadvantaged and the oppressed." The whole person—heart, mind, and conscience—is engaged in and by the world of the poor. That is the distinctive end, the human *telos*, the goal of Jesuit education.

But "this does not make the university a training camp for social activists," by which I take Fr. Kolvenvach to mean that this vision of human solidarity must be integrated and infused into the full range of university programs and into the full range of professional pathways. As Jesuit theologian Jon Sobrino told Mev Puleo, who was worrying about the legitimacy of her work as a photographer, "the world didn't just need liberation theologians but also . . . liberation accountants, architects, writers. And photographers."[24] Clearly, the examples are meant to be suggestive, not exclusive.[25] Or as Dean Brackley, S.J., puts it, "[H]uman beings are made to love, to help others. That is our deepest vocation." But even one person "can have many vocations. I can be a mechanic, an athlete, and a spouse, all at once."[26] Or, as I like to say to my students, there is only one human Vocation—to love God and neighbor (including even our enemy)—but there are many vocations, as many as there are unique human combinations of talents, interests, personalities, and circumstances.

If a whole person of well-educated solidarity with the real world is the end of Jesuit education, what are the means? According to Fr. Kolvenbach, quoting John Paul II (and echoing Gabriel Marcel as well as Pedro Arrupe), "solidarity is learned through 'contact' rather than 'concepts.'" We learn solidarity not through ideas, theories, analyses, or statistics *about* the real world (not that those aren't crucial in a later step), but by personal engagement and encounter *with* it. In what I regard as the two most compelling and insightful sentences of the entire address, Fr. Kolvenbach observes that "when the heart is touched by direct experience, the mind may be challenged to change. Personal involvement with innocent suffering, with the injustice others suffer, is the catalyst for solidarity which then gives rise to intellectual inquiry and moral reflection." To which John Paul II would want us to add, and "a *firm and persevering determination* to commit oneself to the common good." Fr. Kolvenbach neatly sums up the means and ends of Jesuit education in the closing line of this section on "Formation and Learning": "[S]tudents need close involvement with the poor and the marginal now, in order to learn about reality and become adults of solidarity in the future."

Although Fr. Kolvenbach's address will not be treated at non-Jesuit institutions as officially authoritative (as one hopes it is at all Jesuit institutions!), and although some of his language may have a particularly Ignatian saliency, I see no reason why his insights cannot be embraced by all Catholic and even all Christian educators, as well as those from other traditions who collaborate sympathetically and intentionally with them. Indeed, I believe it should be. Those few paragraphs from Fr. Kolvenbach's Santa Clara address offer the basis for a pedagogy to match Catholic social teaching, itself an ethical vision for our times inspired by the Gospel of Jesus Christ.

The Pastoral Circle as Pedagogical

Before moving to a perhaps surprising third chapter, this second chapter has one more task before it. It will help make the important point that the insights of Ignatian pedagogy do not belong to Jesuits and their collaborators alone, but rather to the entire Church, with deep roots in classical antiquity. I have long thought that the well-known "pastoral circle" first articulated in 1980 by Joe Holland and Peter Henriot, S.J., in their seminal little book, *Social Analysis: Linking Faith and Justice*,[27] was at least as pedagogical as pastoral. From an educator's perspective, as well as from a minister's, the circle links faith and justice in a compelling and effective way. But that should not be surprising, since, as is acknowledged in a twenty-fifth anniversary volume, *The Pastoral Circle Revisited: A Critical Quest for Truth and Transformation*,[28] "the original term *circle* was inspired by the 'circle of praxis' as developed by Paulo Freire and the 'hermeneutic circle' as elaborated by [liberation theologian] Juan Luis Segundo."[29] Freire understood praxis to mean "reflection and action upon the world in order to transform it,"[30] that "human beings *are* praxis,"[31] and that *praxis* is therefore at the heart of the educative process:

> Teachers and students (leadership and people), co-intent on reality, are both Subjects, not only in the task of unveiling that reality, and thereby coming to know it critically, but in the task of re-creating that knowledge. As they attain this knowledge of reality through common *reflection and action*, they discover themselves as its permanent re-creators.[32] (emphasis added)

Such a process is circular because "reflection—true reflection—leads to action . . . and that action will constitute an authentic praxis only if its consequences become the object of critical reflection."[33] Indeed, the "circle" may be so tight that "action and reflection occur simultaneously."[34] If the reflection goes deep enough, one might see in this simultaneity the Ignatian ideal captured in the famous phrase, "contemplation in action." One of the goals of Jesuit formation as of Jesuit education generally is that individuals become "contemplatives in action," bringing the Christian vision into contact with the world as it is in order to transform it.

But if the pedigree of the pastoral circle is eminently pedagogical, it is also, in slightly different formulation, historically ecclesial. Thomas Massaro, S.J., reminds us that "the actual process that serves as the basis of all Catholic social teaching is a simple three-step method that most people use almost instinctively every day. This is the process best summarized as see-judge-act."[35] Massaro then directs us to Pope John XXIII's characterization of the process in *Mater et Magistra* (MM; 1961):

> The [church's] teachings in regard to social matters for the most part are put into effect in the following three stages: first, the actual situation is examined; then, the situation is evaluated carefully in relation to these teachings; then only is it decided what can and should be done in order that the traditional norms may be adapted to circumstances of time and place. These three steps are at times expressed by the three words: *observe, judge, act.* (MM 236; emphasis in original)

The pope is referring to the method employed by the Catholic Action movements in the first half of the twentieth century, which Marvin Mich traces to the Belgian priest (later a bishop and Cardinal), Joseph Cardijn. The observe-judge-act "Cardijn method of social analysis and action" was intended for weekly meetings of lay people in Europe but was taken up also in the United States by the Young Christian Workers (YCW) and the Young Christian Students (YCS) in the early 1940s and then in the late 1940s by the Christian Family Movement (CFM).[36] In his commentary on *Quadragesimo Anno* (1931), Mich writes that "Pope Pius XI expected that Catholics would implement his teaching. He especially favored 'Catholic Action' as an *educational program* that would train Catholic leaders—all under the watchful eye of the hierarchy." But as Mich points out, this top-down pedagogy and action plan, at least in the United States, had potential to become more bottom-up because many "expressions of Catholics putting their faith into action: worker priests, liturgy and social justice, *The Catholic Worker*, the Grail, CFM, and more . . . were not directed by the hierarchy but by lay-women and men."[37]

Joe Holland, with Peter Henriot, S.J., the creator of the pastoral circle, extends the history of see-judge-act even further back than the 1930s and its geographical reach beyond Europe and the United States. Cardijn, notes Holland, "was always close to the international Pax Romana lay movement of Catholic Action" at least as early as the 1920s. And Gustavo Gutiérrez, often referred to as the father of liberation theology, "had been a chaplain for Pax Romana in Peru and still remains the official Pax Romana chaplain for Latin America." To complete the intertwining of the origins of the pastoral circle, as Holland points out, "Paulo Freire and the Basic Education movement in Brazil, out of which the first shoots of the basic Christian communities [the pastoral seedbed and expression of liberation theology] emerged, were all rooted in the Brazilian Catholic Action movement."[38]

Holland further notes that Cardijn himself suggested that see-judge-act actually had roots in "the French lay Catholic democratic movement known as Le Sillon (the furrow), . . . with even earlier roots in often marginalized Catholic lay movements" of the mid–nineteenth century.[39] But that's not all. Holland observes "that the structure of papal social encyclicals from 1740 forward generally follows a three-step method quite similar to Cardijn's 'see, judge, act' method and to liberation theology's three moments of social analysis, theological reflection, and pastoral planning." To these three moments Holland and Henriot added, on Henriot's insistence—and happily, from this educator's perspective—the fourth moment of the pastoral circle, "insertion," as a matter of "being self-consciously explicit about our social location."[40] Chapters 4 and 5 are all about this insertion and the unveiling of social location.

But that is *still* not all there is to say about the pedigree of the pastoral circle as an expansion of see-judge-act. Holland traces the same three movements to Aristotelian *phronesis*, or practical reason: "(1) rational-empirical study of reality; (2) articulation of general moral principles of right reason developed from knowledge of reality; and (3) prudential recommendations on how to proceed in action according to right reason within reality." This "approach to social ethics has been dominant in Catholicism to some degree since the time of Aquinas [in the thirteenth century] and almost universally since the time of the Council of Trent" in the mid–sixteenth century.[41]

Figure 2.2 is the diagram of the pastoral circle as presented by Holland and Henriot (*Social Analysis*, p. 8).

The process envisioned is not so much a lock-step progress around the circle as it is an insistence that all four moments be part of any social ministry. Also, because pastoral planning leads to new pastoral action and "insertion," which then creates a new social reality to be analyzed, and so forth, the circle may be better thought of as a "spiral."[42] The analogous caveat should also be extended to the "pedagogical circle" (see Figure 2.3), the pastoral circle as reimagined to outline

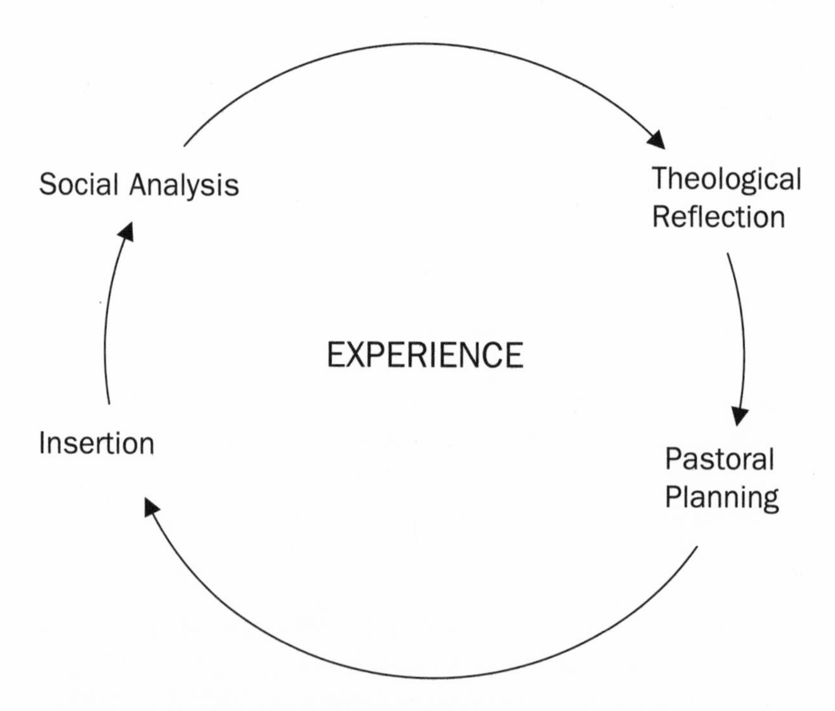

Figure 2.2. The Pastoral Circle

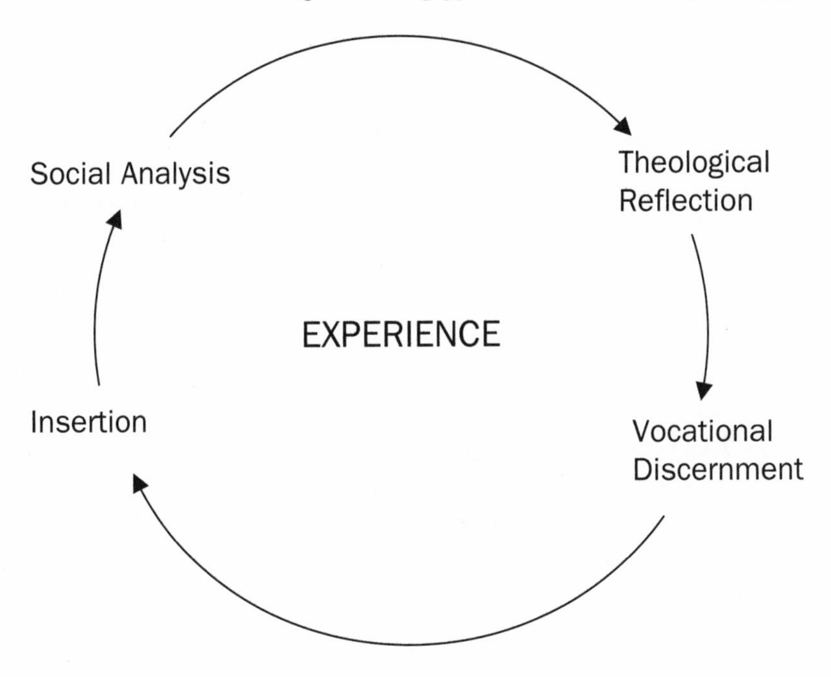

Figure 2.3. The Pedagogical Circle

an educational strategy for Catholic social learning, for the faith that does justice.

The only difference between the two figures, at this level of high generalization, is in the fourth step (the goal of the process), not pastoral planning but rather vocational discernment, to which some attention has already been paid. In each phase of the process, however, means and ends will be appropriately pedagogical. We "insert" or "immerse" students into situations in which they can have "personal encounter" (Marcel) or "vital contact with the reality of injustice" (*Justice in the World*), or "personal involvement with innocent suffering, with the injustices others suffer," so they can "let the gritty reality of this world into their lives, so they can learn to feel it [see Chapter 4 on empathy], think about it critically [social analysis], respond to its suffering [theological reflection], and engage it constructively" [over the course of a lifetime means vocational discernment]

(Kolvenbach). Or, as Fr. Kolvenbach says apropos this distinctively pedagogical fourth step: "The real measure of our Jesuit universities lies in who our students become." I propose that this should be the *distinctive* (if not the exclusive) measure of *any* Catholic or Christian university,[43] and that the pedagogical circle—linked to an Ignatian emphasis on the transformation of the whole person, with Jesus Christ as our *telos* (end or goal), both human model and divine inspiration—is the appropriate means.[44]

But before exploring this pedagogical circle as it is expressed in two pedagogical practices—international immersion (Chapter 4) and domestic service-learning (Chapter 5)—we must make explicit what I believe is implicit in both Catholic social teaching and Ignatian pedagogy: namely, the essential role of schools and educational programs within them as *local counter-cultural communities* of determinative social practice and on-going ethical tradition. Philosopher Alasdair MacIntyre will be our guide.

3 Teaching Justice After MacIntyre

Toward a Catholic Philosophy of Moral Education

> There can be no theory-neutral education into the practice of the virtues.
>
> *Alasdair MacIntyre*

Preamble

Thirty years into a career as a social justice educator, half of that directing and teaching in a Justice and Peace Studies program of a Catholic university, I have come to think of myself as something of an Aristotelian. I have discovered that my understanding of justice pedagogy is better articulated, at least in part, by the *Nicomachean Ethics*[1] than by Lawrence Kohlberg's philosophy[2] and psychology[3] of moral development as inspired by Kant, Piaget, and Rawls. Impressed as I have been by that tradition, it has helped me only marginally to think about how to prepare undergraduates "to be insightful, faithful, lifelong agents for social change whatever their career or profession," as my program professes to do.

Two questions have dominated my reflection: (1) How is a commitment to the difficult work of social justice provoked in the first place? and (2) How is that commitment sustained over a lifetime? The philosopher Gabriel Marcel provides a pointed answer to the first question: "Through personal encounter. Nothing else ever changes anyone in any important way."[4] Want to provoke a new openness to questions of social justice? Then offer opportunities for personal encounter with the victims of injustice.

But after an initial commitment to social justice is born, how do any of us make this a defining pattern of our lives over the long haul?

That would seem to be a matter of character, and that calls our attention to the Aristotelian tradition in ethics, a perspective that Kohlberg early in his career famously dismissed as a relativist "bag of virtues"[5] although he later had second thoughts.[6]

No one, as far as I am aware, provides as much insight into the challenge of the contemporary appropriation of this tradition as Alasdair MacIntyre. Although a moral philosopher rather than a moral educator, MacIntyre's critique of the failure of the Enlightenment Project to construct a rationally based universal ethic, coupled with his critique of the modern nation-state of liberal capitalism as antithetical to the practice of virtue for the common good, provides a challenging if controversial context in which Catholic educators might think about justice pedagogy today. (I will use the terms *moral education* and *justice education* interchangeably.)

This chapter will proceed in five steps, each asking a question. First, *are we all anonymous Aristotelians?* I will outline MacIntyre's argument in his article "Plain Persons and Moral Philosophers"[7] that Aristotelian practical reason is the best tradition of ethical practice available. This chapter recapitulates in highly condensed form some of the much more developed arguments of MacIntyre's major books.[8] I will then ask the question, *how does MacIntyre understand the moral self?* That will introduce an explication of MacIntyre's conception of personal identity as the narrative unity of a life formed by social practices, with their necessary virtues, within a living tradition of moral enquiry. But that raises a further issue about the possibility of virtuous living in our present context, so different from the Greek *polis* (political community) that gave rise to Aristotle's virtue ethics, from which MacIntyre takes inspiration. That takes us to our third question: *Are we all, or should we be, anonymous* revolutionary *Aristotelians?* Here I depend on Kelvin Knight's 1996 article, "Revolutionary Aristotelianism,"[9] which MacIntyre himself[10] recommends as an accurate depiction of his political views, including his belief that the practice of virtue today demands embodiment in local communities of resistance to injustice. But if that is his broad prescription for moral education, *what is MacIntyre's analysis of the actual practice of moral education in America today?* That is the fourth step and final question of this chapter proper.

I pose a fifth question of particular pertinence to educators in the Catholic social teaching tradition: *Can the language of human rights be legitimately preserved as central to programs of justice education despite MacIntyre's claim that human rights are no more real than witches or unicorns?* I draw on the insights of theologian Fr. David Hollenbach, S.J., to answer in the affirmative.

Are We All Anonymous Aristotelians?

MacIntyre means by "plain person" a rational human being concerned for his or her own good who is not a professional moral philosopher.[11] He does point out, however, that in practical life, the moral philosopher continues to be a plain person faced by the same kinds of questions and challenges as anyone else. To the extent that a plain person thinks reflectively about his or good and the human good *per se*, he becomes a moral philosopher, if not a professional theorist. Plain persons need not study the *Nicomachean Ethics* although it is clear that MacIntyre thinks it would be a good idea.

MacIntyre's major thesis is that "plain persons are in fact generally and to a significant degree proto-Aristotelians" (p.138). Here is the key insight. In the ordinary activities of personal, familial, and social life, "one inescapably discovers oneself as a being in norm-governed direction towards goals which are thereby recognized as goods" (pp. 138–39). "These norm-governed directednesses are what Aquinas [a good Aristotelian] calls [inclinations]. . . . [I]t is in virtue of our relationship to these . . . [inclinations], partially defining as they do our nature as human agents, that the precepts of the natural law are so called" (p. 139). That is, if we are paying attention to the intrinsic requirements of human interaction in our ordinary lives, we are learning the precepts of the natural law.

This insight raises two further questions: (1) "how does the plain person make of the ends which are her or his by nature[,] ends actually and rationally directive of her or his activities?" And (2) "in what social contexts do plain persons learn how to order ends rightly and to recognize their mistakes when they have failed to do so?" (p. 139) How does the natural law come to be recognized and intelligently practiced? We do so through being taught by those more expert than ourselves how to pay attention to and how to think about our activities. According to MacIntyre

> It is through initiation into the ordered relationships of some particular practice or practices, through education into the skills and virtues which it or they require, and through an understanding of the relationship of those skills and virtues to the achievement of the goods internal to that practice or those practices that we first find application in everyday life for just such a teleological scheme of understanding as that which Aristotle presents at a very different level of philosophical sophistication in the *Nicomachean Ethics* . . . . [W]e . . . become evidently, even if unwittingly, Aristotelians. (p. 140)

We learn by doing and by reflecting on that doing in concert with others. That doing MacIntyre calls a *practice*, which he defines (rather laboriously) as

> . . . any coherent and complex form of socially established cooperative human activity through which goods internal to that form of activity are realized in the course of trying to achieve those standards of excellence which are appropriate to, and partially definitive of, that form of activity, with the result that human powers to achieve excellence, and human conceptions of the ends and goods involved, are systematically extended.[12]

Practices, that is, foster the virtues necessary to achieve specific human goods. Reflection on such practices and their vagaries is integral to moral development and human achievement.

What we learn from such reflection is to make two crucial distinctions. First, we learn to distinguish what pleases me here and now from what makes for excellence in pursuit of the goods internal to the practice in which I am engaged. Second, we learn to distinguish what is good unqualifiedly from what is good for me here and now at this stage of my moral progress. Clearly, there is a reflexive dynamism or dialectic at work here, one suggested by Aristotle's definition of virtue,[13] which invokes both "the mean *relative to us*" (emphasis added) at this particular stage of our development and "the man of practical wisdom"—the virtuous person *in the ideal* who has achieved or is achieving his *telos* (purpose or goal). As MacIntyre puts it, "through a process of learning, making mistakes, correcting those mistakes and so moving towards the achievement of excellence, the individual comes to understand her or himself as *in via*, in the middle of a journey" (p. 140). That journey, as we have seen in Aristotle's perspective itself, is a developmental project.

Or rather, the individual comes to understand her or himself as simultaneously in the middle of various journeys because "no individual lives her or his life wholly within the confines of any one practice" (p. 140). How are the goods of these various practices to be ordered? What is the supreme good that relativizes all other goods? That is, the plain person will, "from time to time, . . . retrospectively examine . . . what her or his life amounts to as a whole" and so will ask, " 'to what conception of my overall good have I so far committed myself? And, do I now have reason to put it in question?' " Each of us is a protagonist in "a story whose outcome can be success or failure." It is "in terms of the outcomes of particular narratives about particular lives" that "the conception of a *telos* of human life is generally first comprehended" (p. 141). We move from the particular stories that make up a life to the overall story that *is* a life, and then to the universal story that is human life *per se*.

In such retrospective self-examination, as plain persons, "we characteristically draw upon resources provided by some stock stories from which we had earlier learned to understand both our own lives and the lives of others in narrative terms, the oral and written literature of whatever particular culture it is that we happen to inhabit" (p. 141). A cultural tradition provides us with a theory of the *telos* of human life that demands our allegiance over against rival traditions. Thus we have arrived at what John Horton and Susan Mendus[14] describe as the three central concepts of MacIntyre's moral theory: (1) the narrative and therefore teleological self engaged in (2) social practices with their attendant goods and virtues as understood in the context of (3) a living tradition of moral enquiry. The first of these three concepts is especially relevant to the present discussion and so deserves further analysis.

How Does MacIntyre Understand the Moral Self?

It is a "central thesis" for MacIntyre that "man is in his actions and practice, as well as in his fictions, a story-telling animal. . . . [for] I can only answer the question 'What am I to do?' if I can answer the prior question 'Of what story or stories do I find myself a part?' And what the narrative concept of selfhood requires is . . . twofold. On the one hand, . . . I am the *subject* of a history that is my own and no one else's."[15] And "to be the subject of a narrative that runs from one's birth to one's death is . . . to be accountable for the actions and experiences which compose a narratable life" (p. 217). On the other hand, "I am not only accountable, I am one who can always ask others for an account, who can put others to the question." And what is the question to which each of us must fashion an answer through the narratives of our lives? "'What is the good for man?'" indicates "a narrative quest" that "is always an education both as to the character of that which is sought and in self-knowledge" (pp. 218–19). This perspective on the narrative unity of a human life suggests a new definition of the virtues:

> The virtues therefore are to be understood as those dispositions which will not only sustain practices and enable us to achieve the goods internal to practices, but which will sustain us in the relevant kind of quest for the good, by enabling us to overcome the harms, dangers, temptations and distractions which we encounter, and which will furnish us with increasing self-knowledge and increasing knowledge of the good. (p. 219)

The virtues are necessary to particular practices within a life but also to the unity of that life as a whole. This brings Macintyre to a "provisional" answer to his fundamental question: "the good life for man [*sic*] is the life spent in seeking for the good life for man, and the virtues necessary for the seeking are those which will enable us to understand what more and what else the good life for man is" (p. 219).

Michael Fuller recapitulates "the basic structure of MacIntyre's 'narrative unity' argument" as follows:

> (1) We should . . . drop Aristotle's and Aquinas's "metaphysical biology," since it has been discredited by modern science. . . . (2) . . . [W]e can retain the intelligibility of the idea of a *telos* for human life by suggesting that each human being can and must provide their own *telos* by "telling themselves a story" about their own life. . . . (3) But, in practice, each individual's story interlocks with other individuals' stories. (4) A principal form of such interlocking is through the shared story or stories which membership of the same tradition provides. . . . (5) Such narrative intelligibility . . . is an essential ingredient of having any concrete sense of personal, intellectual and moral identity. . . . (6) But, in practice, the modern self is confronted by a welter of competing traditions. . . . (7) [T]here are principally three such competing traditions: (Aristotelian/Thomist) Tradition, Encyclopaedia, and Genealogy [[16]]. (8) Therefore, if we can effectively argue the case for the greater coherence of . . . [the first] of these competing narratives. . . . [w]e can . . . restore a fairly definitive *telos*, identity, and "narrative unity" to the bewildered modern self.[17]

In sum, for MacIntyre, there can be no coherent personal moral identity apart from participation in a tradition of social practices and moral enquiry. We are all anonymous Aristotelians because "every human being . . . lives out her or his life in a narrative form which is structured in terms of a *telos*, of virtues and of rules in an Aristotelian mode."[18] It is, of course, possible for a person to fail to learn and to practice well this Aristotelian mode. Indeed, it is MacIntyre's indictment of modern moral philosophy specifically and modern culture generally that each has fostered such failure. One of MacIntyre's (p. 61) essential complaints against modernity is that "when the distinctively modern self was invented. . . . what was invented was the individual," and that "the self thus conceived . . . is now thought of as criterionless, because the kind of *telos* in terms of which it once judged and acted is no longer thought to be credible" (p. 33). We live "after virtue." The typically modern self has no "home" (tradition) in which to learn the virtues. But to the extent that we engage in social practices governed by norms that point toward goods internal to those practices and which can only be achieved through the development of the relevant virtues, and to the extent that such practices compel us to reflect on how those goods are to be ordered relative to our overall good and to the good for humans *per se*, as well as to the extent that we come to understand that we can only answer such questions in terms of a living tradition, to that extent we are all, however unwittingly, proto-Aristotelians. But that answers only our first two questions. What is MacIntyre's fuller analysis of the contextual challenges facing the education of the moral self into the virtues? In a word, what are MacIntyre's politics?

Are We All Anonymous Revolutionary Aristotelians?

As mentioned, I rely on Kelvin Knight's 1996 article, "Revolutionary Aristotelianism," for an accurate summary of MacIntyre's political views. Knight begins with a review of MacIntyre's moral theory and his critique of other theories, which he sums up this way: "Aristotelianism is . . . less a particular (syllogistic) conception of practical rationality than the general rationality of practices as such, in contrast with which all other rationalities may be described as ideologies."[19] Although the point is not elaborated, Knight makes this interesting observation on MacIntyre's behalf: "Aristotelianism is the tradition of the moral theory of practice that has developed in the West, but other civilizations have other such traditions" (p. 889).

We begin to move outward from MacIntyre's analysis of practices as such with the following distinction: "'Practices must not be confused with institutions.'" (p. 889). Medicine is a practice; a hospital is an institution. Institutions are concerned with money, power, and status. Institutions make practices possible; but whereas practices tend to be cooperative, institutions tend to be competitive. "'In this context,'" in MacIntyre's own words, "'the essential function of the virtues is clear. Without them, without justice, courage and truthfulness, practices could not resist the corrupting power of institutions'"

(p. 889). Money, power, and status are what MacIntyre calls "goods external to practices" (p. 889). There is an inevitable tension between the goods internal to and the goods external to practices. How that tension is played out depends upon the culture. Institutions should serve practices, and internal goods should be honored more than external goods, however necessary those external goods are to the practices.

"In the post-Enlightenment world, however, the reverse rationale has increasingly prevailed. Both capitalist corporations and states are structured in the same, bureaucratic way." And the managerial reasoning common to both " 'entails the obliteration of any distinction between manipulative and non-manipulative social relations' by denying the reality of the latter" (p. 890). Management, from MacIntyre's point of view, "is a mere technique, not a practice with goods internal to itself," so that in the characteristic institutions of modern culture, what MacIntyre calls the "goods of effectiveness" are more highly valued than the "goods of excellence." This "moral error" is at the heart of MacIntyre's critique of modernity (p. 891). This moral reversal is particularly apparent in MacIntyre's comments on the identification of *pleonexia* (acquisitiveness) as a vice in Aristotelian theory and as a virtue in capitalist cultures. In the former, work is understood as a practice whose rewards are primarily internal to it, while in the latter, work is undertaken primarily to acquire external goods. Given the pervasive entrenchment of such a moral reversal, what is to be done?

According to Knight, MacIntyre believes that " 'the problem is not to reform the dominant order, but to find ways for local communities to survive by sustaining a life of the common good against the disintegrating forces of the nation-state and the market' " (p. 894). "Accordingly, the tasks for a politics in the Aristotelian tradition are to defend the rationality, ideals, creativity and cooperative care for common goods of practices against institutional corruption and managerial manipulation, and to uphold internal goods of excellence against external goods and claims of effectiveness" (p. 895). In this context, MacIntyre indicates what role the university might play in such an Aristotelian politics. "The 'peculiar and [socially] essential function' of universities is, now, to be 'places where . . . the wider society [can] learn how to conduct its own debates . . . in a rationally defensible way'" (p. 895). MacIntyre's politics is obviously revolutionary in a very particular way. There seem to be no barricades, not even metaphorical ones, in sight.

On the other hand, in the Introduction to the revised edition of *Marxism and Christianity*, MacIntyre argues that "an adequate regard for justice always involves not only a concern that justice be done and injustice prevented or remedied on any particular occasion, but also resistance to and, *where possible, the abolition of institutions that systematically generate injustice*."[20] Where possible (which may be a very limiting qualification), MacIntyre does indeed seem to envision reform of the dominant order through the abolition of unjust institutions. Just how broad an agenda this might be is indicated by his subsequent assertion that "capitalism . . . provides systematic incentives to develop a type of character that has a propensity to injustice."[21] But then he draws back from that potentially more revolutionary agenda by urging that "the need" is "to construct and sustain practice-based forms of local participatory community that will be able to survive the insidious and destructive pressure of contemporary capitalism and of the modern state."[22] But what does that mean for the social practice that is moral education?

What Is MacIntyre's Analysis of Moral Education in America Today?

What MacIntyre has written about in "Aquinas's Critique of Education" might well represent his Aristotelian perspective on contemporary American education:

> Where for Aquinas education presupposes a background of shared moral beliefs, the dominant educational ideals of contemporary America presuppose a morally heterogeneous and divided society. Where for Aquinas the goal of education is the achievement of a comprehensive and completed understanding, in modern America what education offers are skills and knowledge designed to enable the student to pursue the satisfaction of her or his preferences, whatever—within certain very wide limits—they

> may be. And where for Aquinas what the individual is to be measured by, in education as elsewhere, is her or his success or failure in directing her- or himself towards *the* human good, the dominant culture of the American present takes it for granted that there is no such thing as *the* human good, but that each individual must at some point choose for her- or himself among a variety of different and rival conceptions of the good. A good education is then an education that prepares individuals for making such choices. And by that standard a Thomist education is a bad education.[23]

And by that same contemporary standard a truly *Aristotelian* moral education is a bad education. Given the current popularity of character education programs in the United States, MacIntyre's critique of American education might seem not only unduly harsh but simply off the mark. In fact, without ever using the term "character education," MacIntyre provides a devastating critique in his wryly titled essay, "How to seem virtuous without actually being so."[24] An examination of that essay will help us put Aristotelian moral education in critical tension with the actual practice of the preferred mode of character education in America today, which often claims an Aristotelian pedigree.[25]

In "How to seem virtuous without actually being so," MacIntyre argues for two conclusions. The first is that not all virtue-concepts are created equal. Any rationally defensible account must distinguish between genuine and counterfeit virtues. Second, because our society includes "a number of rival and incompatible accounts of the virtues . . . , there can be no rationally defensible shared programme for moral education for our society as such, but only a number of rival and conflicting programmes, each from the standpoint of one specific contending view" (p. 118). If modern moral philosophy and culture is "after virtue," *a fortiori* modern moral education is "after" virtue education. But "the proponents of shared public moral education," who are "enormously influential . . . , insist to the contrary that we do in fact share a morality" (p. 118). How does MacIntyre refute this claim for a commonplace morality?

According to MacIntyre (p. 119), any "tolerably systematic and coherent understanding of the virtues" must answer four questions. The first concerns "counterfactual judgments." If I judge an act to be virtuous, to what judgments am I necessarily committed in other circumstances? Judgments of virtue must arise out of a reasonably comprehensive and not merely *ad hoc* or spontaneous perspective, if they are to be rationally defensible. "A second [and not logically independent] question concerns the type of reason for acting as he or she does which is ascribed in judging that someone is brave or generous or just" (p. 119). One of the differences between genuine and counterfeit virtues is the difference between right and wrong reasons for one and the same action. One might perform a courageous act to save another person's life or to call attention to oneself as courageous. Intentions reveal reasons, and not all reasons are created morally equal. A third question is closely related to the second: "what was it, both in the situation and the action, which pleased or pained the agent?" (p. 120). We are reminded that the virtuous person, according to Aristotle [Ross; 1104b],[26] will be pleased or pained in the right way at the right things. MacIntyre's fourth and final question that all rationally defensible accounts of the virtues must answer is "what range of different types of situation provides a sufficient warrant for such an ascription of a virtue to that individual?" (p. 121) This question emphasizes the need for a systematic and comprehensive account of the virtues, including regard for each of the concerns raised by the three previous questions.

MacIntyre argues that "the answers supplied by commonplace usage are highly indeterminate" (p. 121). Any shared public program of moral education will necessarily be open and thin if it is to claim allegiance within a heterogeneous and divided society. Indeed, "what our contemporary political culture requires from those who claim public and political authority is an appearance of virtue congruent with the rhetoric of shared values. And both the appearance and that rhetoric are well served by the indeterminancy of the virtue-concepts of contemporary commonplace usage" (p. 122). It is important to note that MacIntyre is not arguing that it is impossible for individuals ever to act virtuously in contemporary society but that a publicly supported program of moral education is unlikely to foster genuine virtue as a matter of course. It is more likely that individuals will, through no fault of their own, learn to seem virtuous without actually being so. Genuine virtues, as we have seen MacIntyre argue previously, depend on social practices aimed at genuine human goods within living traditions of moral enquiry into the human good *per se*. Such traditions provide highly determinate answers to MacIntyre's four questions. And that determinancy can presently be found only in local communities that are counter-cultural. The culture to which they are counter, of course, is precisely that culture in which a commonplace rhetoric of shared morality can produce only counterfeit virtues.

MacIntyre's second conclusion toward which his argument moves concerns moral education more directly. "All education into the virtues, especially the education of the young, has to begin by discovering some way of transforming the motivations of those who are to be so educated" (p. 123). The problem faced by moral educators "is how to enable their pupils to come to value goods just as and insofar as they are goods, and virtues just as and insofar as they are virtues" (p. 123). But it is exactly this motivation and this valuation that a thin, open, and indeterminate commonplace moral education cannot systematically produce. Again, "graduates" of such a program may occasionally "do what a genuinely virtuous person would do . . . , but because they have misidentified what it is about these actions that would make them genuine examples of some particular virtue, they will extrapolate falsely in making inferences as to what the virtues require in situations other than those with which they were at first familiarized" (p. 123). The crucial difference is that "true judgments about what virtues are required in some particular situation, . . . always either presuppose or are explicitly derived from some conception of the human *telos* as being the achievement of a type of life of which the virtues are necessary constitutive parts" (p. 124). It is precisely this *telos* that a shared public program of moral education in a heterogeneous society cannot agree on, perhaps even argue constructively about. As MacIntyre has agued, "the American present takes for granted that there is no such thing as *the* human good."[27] And as "there is no theory-neutral, pre-philosophical, yet adequately determinate account of the virtues. . . . so it also becomes clear that there can be no theory-neutral education into the practice of the virtues" (p. 126).

We have previously explicated MacIntyre's argument that "Aristotelianism is . . . at odds with the standpoint of the established economic systems of advanced modernity" (p. 128). He now argues "that this is so strengthens [his] claim that there is no non-controversial stance to be taken on the virtues, and that this is so in a way and to a degree that makes it impossible for there to be a single shared public system of moral education with determinate and substantive moral content" (p. 128). From MacIntyre's Aristotelian perspective, moral education as a social practice conducive to the development of virtue can only be genuine within local communities alternative and resistant to the counterfeit morality of commonplace rhetoric. It is not too strong to say that for MacIntyre, there is a real possibility that the modern self as such cannot be a fully realized moral self. A fractured *polis* militates against the integration of the self into a coherent tradition of virtuous living. The education of the moral self can only be practiced in opposition to the social conditions of post-Enlightenment managerial, acquisitive individualism. If "the barbarians . . . have already been governing us for quite some time,"[28] moral educators must sit up, take notice, and respond accordingly. They may be the new St. Benedicts that MacIntyre is awaiting.[29]

This, then, is the framework that MacIntyre provides in which to think about education for justice in Catholic education today. If the crucial question we must ask ourselves is how to form our students to be "insightful, faithful, lifelong agents for social change whatever their career or profession," then MacIntyre offers a compelling and challenging answer: We justice educators must be at least countercultural if not revolutionary Aristotelians. A few further questions come quickly to mind. What are the social practices that structure our courses, programs, and curricula? What are the virtues necessary to those practices? How does our Catholic, Christian heritage provide a determinate narrative that ultimately forms our ideal of the persons we and our students are meant to become? In a world of gross injustice, violence, and suffering, what is the human *telos* that informs our teaching, learning, research, and way of proceeding? For my own part, as the director of a Justice and Peace Studies program at a Catholic university, no one has provoked me to think more deeply about my own practice than Alasdair MacIntyre.

MacIntyre, Human Rights, and Catholic Social Teaching

There is one major obstacle, however, to a Catholic justice educator's full embrace of a MacIntyrian perspective, and that is his dismissal of the language of human rights, which is for him an expression of that commonplace morality: in this case, a morality with global pretensions that can produce no genuine virtue. In this coda, I'd like to attempt to remove, or at least reduce the size of, that obstacle. I do so by posing and answering a fifth question: *Can the language of human rights be legitimately preserved as central to programs of justice education despite MacIntyre's claim that human rights are no more real than witches or unicorns?*[30] Here I make use of an article by Fr. David Hollenbach, S.J., titled "A communitarian reconstruction of human rights: contributions from Catholic tradition."[31] That tradition is, in MacIntyre's own terms, my first native language of morality. I have tried, however recently and incompletely, to make MacIntyre my second native language, as represented in this chapter. What remains is to translate, with Hollenbach's help, between the two languages, to speak human rights, as it were, in a MacIntyrian dialect.

Hollenbach begins with this arresting observation: "During the last century and a half, the Roman Catholic church has moved from strong opposition to the rights championed by liberal thinkers of the eighteenth and nineteenth centuries to the position of one of the leading institutional advocates for human rights on the world stage today" (p. 127). How can this dramatic moral reversal be explained? Hollenbach's thesis is that

> The pivot on which this reconstruction [of human rights] turns is the traditional natural-law conviction that the human person is an essentially social being. Catholic thought and action in the human rights sphere, in other words, are rooted in a communitarian alternative to liberal human rights theory. Because of this stress on the communal rather than the

> individualist grounding of rights, contemporary Catholic discussions of constitutional democracy and free-market capitalism diverge in notable ways from the liberal theories of rights that are regnant today. (p. 128)

To quote *Gaudium et Spes* (1965), one of the major documents of the Second Vatican Council, because "God's plan gives man's vocation a communitarian nature," "more than an individualistic ethic is required."[32] It is against this background of communitarian anthropology that Hollenbach remarks that "the most pointed objection to human rights theory on Aristotelian-Thomistic grounds is that of Alasdair MacIntyre" (p. 129).

MacIntyre assumes that because human rights are framed as universal by Enlightenment philosophy and post-Enlightenment liberalism that they are necessarily therefore at odds with community and the common good. If that assumption were true, Catholicism and human rights would have to part company. But that this assumption is mistaken can be seen by even a cursory review of Pope John XXIII's great encyclical, *Pacem in Terris* (*Peace on Earth*; PT; 1963),[33] in which the common good and human rights are explicitly linked and even defined in terms of one another. John famously defines the common good as "the sum total of those conditions of social living whereby men are enabled to achieve their own integral perfection more fully and easily" (PT #58). In their 1986 pastoral letter *Economic Justice for All*, the U.S. Catholic bishops further refine this tradition by defining human rights as the "minimum conditions for life in community."[34] As Hollenbach puts it, "understood this way, rights language does not presuppose an individualistic view of the person. . . . It begins rather with a discussion of the 'responsibilities of social living'" (p. 141), a contemporary articulation of the biblical imperative to love one's neighbor.

Having articulated this communitarian ethic of human rights, Hollenbach then considers the charge that is sometimes leveled against MacIntyre: namely, that his emphasis on local community and tradition makes him a relativist. MacIntyre's own rebuttal has been to argue for intellectual engagement between rival traditions toward more adequate formulations of truth. Traditions must be open to correction through encounter with other traditions. But according to Hollenbach, MacIntyre "has failed so far to reflect sufficiently on the institutional implications of his commitment to inquiry as constitutive of any tradition that is in working order." But if he is to follow through on this commitment, "he *must* endorse rights such as freedom of speech and religion. Without these rights, participation in inquiry must come to an end. . . . MacIntyre's animus against the idea of human rights is self-contradictory" (pp. 143–44; emphasis in original). The creation of the virtuous community, says Hollenbach, depends upon the acknowledgement of human rights beyond one's own community of practice and inquiry. We learn the natural law language of universal human rights through authentic encounter with those outside our immediate communities of discourse.

Within Catholic tradition, it is no contradiction to organize a moral education program with an emphasis on social justice defined in terms of universal human rights *and* to think of that program as fostering a community of students and teachers mutually engaged in learning what it means to practice the virtues over a lifetime of social engagement. That second dimension makes us, as MacIntyre would say, revolutionary Aristotelians. But that hardly precludes us from being counter-cultural Catholic Christians committed to universal human rights. Indeed, it demands it.

A Modest Example

Practice flowing from this educational philosophy obviously cannot be limited to the occasional or even regular lesson plan devoted to the various dimensions of Catholic morality. In MacIntyre's vision, it is the ongoing, self-critical moral life of the community as a whole, rooted in a living tradition, which forms and educates each successive generation. In this last section, I offer a brief example of how that vision might be embodied in the curricular content and pedagogical structure of a university course.

"Faith and Moral Development," a course in the Justice and Peace Studies Program at Creighton University, is innovative in at least two ways. First, although it is a three-credit-hour course, it consists of three one-credit, student-led seminars over three semesters. Although the individual seminar rosters vary, there is enough consistency of membership, format, and purpose that students do, I believe, develop a modest sense of community, of shared commitment to social justice and to a spirituality to support that commitment over the long haul. Second, students take turns leading the discussion of writings by or about moral exemplars such as Dorothy Day; Martin Luther King, Jr.; Oscar Romero; and the villagers of Le Chambon, France, who rescued Jewish children from the Nazi war machine during World War II. In addition to case studies that give students a glimpse of an heroic legacy, we also consider various theoretical perspectives (psychological, philosophical, theological, sociological) on the faith and moral development of such exemplars, who provide diverse but compelling images and narratives of the human *telos* so important to MacIntyre's Aristotelian vision. (Chapter 6 offers further analysis of the rationale for such a course.)

I was prompted, while reading MacIntyre, to reflect on my much earlier intuition of the necessity of such a course to the Justice and Peace Studies Program. That has led me to think of myself, in practice and now also in theory, as something of an Aristotelian. That in turn explains the impetus behind this chapter and why I believe that Catholic educators at all levels have much to learn from MacIntyre about teaching justice in our present cultural and historical circumstances.

PART II APPLICATIONS

4 Immersion, Empathy, and Perspective Transformation

Semestre Dominicano, 1998

No dije que sería facil. Dije que valdría la peña.
(I didn't say it would be easy. I said it would be worth the pain.)

Wall placard in Hogar Luby, an orphanage for handicapped children in the Dominican Republic

This chapter is dedicated to all the participants of *Semestre Dominicano* (1992–2003) and *Encuentro Dominicano* (2005–present), but especially to the students, faculty, and staff of SD Spring 1998.

Theology in the Pit of the Stomach

On Good Friday, 1998, 15 Creighton University undergraduates, two professors and their two teenage children, the program director and his assistant, with two guide/interpreters, participated in a uniquely powerful version of the traditional Catholic devotional practice: the Stations of the Cross. The usual location for this Lenten activity is the nave of a church with its 14 depictions of Jesus' journey to Calvary. As devotees circumambulate the church's interior, each scene is described, a prayer said or song intoned, a silence embraced.

I was one of those professors, and the venue for our Stations of the Cross was the crowded, trash-ridden streets of Port-au-Prince, the capital city of Haiti. It had taken us more than 12 hours to negotiate the 250 roundabout miles (and the border crossing) from Santiago, Dominican Republic (DR), where we were engaged in the Creighton University's College of Arts and Sciences semester abroad program, housed at the Creighton-affiliated Institute for Latin American Concern (ILAC). In another sense, it had taken our group three months to reach this destination. Since our introduction in mid-January to the reality of the developing world as experienced in the DR, we had been working up to this trip to Haiti—easily the most undeveloped, most miserable nation in the Western Hemisphere.

Semestre Dominicano (Dominican Semester), as the program was called,[1] combined academics, community service, cultural immersion, spirituality, and other dimensions. The goal was not only to garner critical knowledge of the world but also personal growth and even moral transformation. Our Holy Week trip to Haiti embodied much of what makes the program, for many students, "my best semester."

Worse Than This?

As Creighton professor of Latin American history Richard Super aptly put it, the contrast between the DR and Haiti can seem as great as that between the United States and the DR.[2] As community service, two of our students had been spending one day and night each week in a Haitian *batey* (agricultural workers' community) outside Santiago. All of us had visited the *batey* at least once. Conditions there were so poor—for example, six latrines for as many as 900 people—we couldn't imagine how they could be attractive enough to draw Haitians from the other side of the island.

On that Good Friday, in Port-au-Prince, we found out.

Led by Ron Voss, an American who had joined his lot over many years to that of the Haitian people, we made our tour of their recent tragic and brutal history. Our first stop was St. John Bosco Church, where a prophetic young "priest of the poor," Fr. Jean Bertrand Aristide—later *President* Aristide—had made a reputation in the 1980s by speaking out against the human rights abuses of successive Haitian governments. Preaching liberation theology, Aristide had become the eloquent voice of the voiceless poor, and his church had become their hope and refuge.[3]

Ron informed us that before Sunday mass was to begin on September 11, 1988, Aristide was warned that government thugs were on their way to the church. After consulting with worshippers who had already arrived, Fr. Aristide went ahead with the celebration of the Eucharist. The gang arrived, scaled the walls around the church, and attacked the congregation with machetes, firearms—and fire. Thirteen people were killed, many others were wounded, and the building itself was torched. Roofless, gutted, and weed-infested, St. John Bosco Church still stood in 1998 as a solemn monument to the courage and faith—and suffering—of the Haitian people.

After we had taken in this story, we got back into our van to make our way to the next "station." I casually remarked, "That sure gets theology down out of the clouds." One of the students (a "hard" science major, now completing his medical training) responded, without missing a beat, "Yeah, right into the pit of your stomach."

Context Is Everything

To a professor who fears that theology may mean little more to students than a course to be endured on the way to a degree and a career, this rejoinder was revelation. The insight was at least twofold. First, theological ideas have real consequences in the lives of ordinary, even illiterate, people. While formal theological study may be for the privileged few (such as professors and their captive-audience students), it ought to be undertaken with a view to its real-world ramifications.

Second, in education, especially an education inspired by a commitment to "the promotion of justice," context is everything. As one of the students remarked in a final paper, "I can't imagine taking this course [an introduction to Christology] in Omaha. It just wouldn't have been the same. It wouldn't have meant so much." Another student explained why. On Good Friday, she said, we had encountered Christ himself in the crucified people of Haiti (see Matthew 25:36–41). Just what is this pedagogical context that makes such a difference?

What the eye doesn't see, doesn't move the heart (Haitian proverb)

Christian educator Russell Butkus has described the key to conscientization succinctly and insightfully. "Any hope of sponsoring people to critical consciousness and social action is directly related to their capacity to reflect on experiences and situations that *deeply* touch their lives."[4] The process of conscientization in a faith context depends upon what I outline in Chapter 2 as the Pedagogical Circle, consisting of (1) personal encounter with the poor, (2) analysis of their situation and its structural causes, (3) theological reflection (Where is God to be found, and what does God call us to do?), and (4) a commitment to intelligent and responsible action. All this happens best in a community of support. *Semestre Dominicano* provided all these ingredients through its various components.

The obvious difference between Freire's conscientization and that of *Semestre Dominicano* is the student. Freire sought to empower illiterate poor adults in a Third World setting by teaching them to read their world while learning to read the word. *Semestre Dominicano* sought, one might say, to "disempower" educated, privileged young adults, citizens of an affluent superpower, by creating a context in which heart-breaking personal relationships with the poor seem to necessitate personal transformation. It is fair to say that most of the scores of students who have participated in *Semestre Dominicano* would describe their four months in the Dominican Republic not only as their best semester—as the semester in which they learned the most—but as "life-changing," a genuinely transformative and watershed event in their lives.

Interpreting the Experience

Two essays in the 1987 book *Pedagogies for the Non-Poor* had previously alerted me to what other U.S. justice educators believed to be the essential elements of such programs. William Bean Kennedy argues that "most of the problems faced in education for transformation of the non-poor must deal with the ideological blinders within which and the ideological filters through which they perceive and interpret their world and what goes on it."[5] Moral reasoning, at whatever level or stage, does not take place in a vacuum. What we see depends on where we stand. Advanced or "postconventional" moral judgment[6] may mean the ability to take multiple perspectives on moral issues, but that is no guarantee against the unconscious bias of social position.

David Moshman, in his essay "The Construction of Moral Rationality" speaks to this dimension of the development of moral cognition:

> . . . most people in most cultures associate almost exclusively with people who share, if not their specific moralities, at least their core metaethical commitments [how they *think about* moral beliefs]. Disequilibration at this level is likely to come less from daily social life than from *extended engagement with others in situations of personal crisis, cultural conflict, or rigorous intellectual exchange.*[7]

Almost everything was new, different, and difficult for U.S. students in their first weeks in the DR: living arrangements, food, language, socioeconomic context, intense and constant community life, distance from family and friends, and so forth.[8] At this stage of the program, the director reported, not entirely facetiously, everybody wants to go home. *Personal crises*, Moshman's first condition for disequilibration (disturbance of normal patterns of perception and thinking) came with the territory.

A student from a later semester group wrote compellingly, in a reflection for one of my courses after her return to Omaha, about the profoundly disorienting, but somehow not frightening, experience of her first night with her hosts in a rural village, her *campo* family:

> I had the most curious experience that first night I was there, when my host sister blew out the candle in our room and I was all of a sudden plunged into complete darkness. Talk about ontological insecurity! I could feel that I was lying on "my bed," but other than that, I felt like I could have been anywhere or nowhere. I had no sights, no sounds, and I didn't even have my language; I was thinking in simple Spanish sentences. I had lost all points of reference. I quieted my thoughts and for a moment I experienced the most complete stillness. From there I began to work my way back into more complex English thoughts, examined my day with amazement, and touched the wall to reassure myself of the material existence of myself and the world! The challenge that I was more aware

> of for the rest of the semester was to balance how much of my "formed" self I brought to life and how much I struck out into a new way of being.[9]

Furthermore, from arrival to departure, students were confronted with different values, perspectives, attitudes, customs, and lifestyles. As one student amusingly put it, "I found myself in a strange new world. What was going on here? Do these people actually use words, or is it simply an unintelligible slur that is somehow considered a language?" She felt this strangeness especially at her service site, a school: "I did not know what was expected of me, what I was supposed to teach or how I was supposed to teach it. I became frustrated with my inability and inexperience as a teacher, and most of all with my language skills." Although many of the students developed a fond appreciation for many dimensions of Dominican culture, *cultural conflict*, Moshman's second condition, was at the crux of the experience.

The *intellectual exchange* of the classroom was not only as *rigorous* as it would have been on our home campus,[10] but it was also much more immediately energized by its social and cultural context. *Semestre Dominicano* was in many ways a classroom without walls or clocks. Finally, these three elements—personal crisis, cultural conflict, and intellectual exchange—all took place in a context of "extended engagement with others." In this case, the "others" included not only instructors and fellow students, but most importantly, the Dominican people, most of them greatly impoverished relative to the families of our students.

Toward a Pedagogy of Transformation

Kennedy offers the following structural elements of an educational program that would take the ideological factor seriously. The characterization of each element is my own paraphrase.

A. Commitment of time and energy (personal investment, no quick fixes)
B. Radical change of environment (getting out of our "comfort zone")

C. Risk (no vulnerability, no movement—so get the adrenalin running)
D. Community support (sharing the risk, encouraging the change)
E. Reflection (personal, communal, ethical, philosophical, theological)
F. "Data" from outside (stories from "the other," social analysis)[11]

Robert Evans, also in *Pedagogies for the Non-Poor*, offers an overlapping list of "components of transformation:"

A. Encounter with the poor (radical change of environment)
B. Experiential immersion that challenges assumptions (radical change of environment)
C. Openness to vulnerability (risk)
D. Community of support and accountability (community support)
E. Vision and values (reflection)
F. Serious, critical, systemic socioeconomic analysis (data from outside)
G. Commitment, involvement, leadership (commitment of time and energy)
H. Symbol, ritual, liturgy (perhaps included in reflection)[12]

I believe that all these elements were included in *Semestre Dominicano*, accounting for its consistently transformative effects in its student participants.

Previous to my own involvement in the program, I had developed an interest because of what former participants had to say about it. The several who took my ethics courses seemed not to be able to write a paper or carry on a discussion on almost any topic without referring to their DR experience. By their own admission, their perspectives had been changed. So I volunteered to be an accompanying professor and made plans to do a qualitative research case study. Hoping to trace, articulate, and analyze what seemed to be a remarkably effective educational process, I developed or gathered four types of documents about the students' experiences over that four-month period.

The first type consists of approximately one-hour interviews with three groups of four or five students (14 participants total) three times during the semester: shortly after arrival, near the midpoint of the semester, and two weeks before departure. Interviews were audio taped and transcribed. The second type of document comprises personal journals written at my request but with varying frequency, regularity, and focus by nine students. A third type of document consists of 25 short academic papers containing personal reflection, that I, the students, or one of the other instructors thought would be relevant to my project. The last category of data is my own field-notes: observations recorded throughout the four-month period. These four sources produced almost 600 pages of data. I have also taught many other students who have participated in *Semestre Dominicano* in subsequent years and who have written compellingly of their experiences in academic papers and personal reflections; I also draw upon these writings.

Empathy, Marginality, and Young Adult Moral Development

To provide some focus on an otherwise unwieldy mass of data, I will use the theoretical perspective of psychologist Martin Hoffman, as articulated in his career-capping book, *Empathy and Moral Development*, in which empathy is defined as "the involvement of psychological processes that make a person have feelings that are more congruent with another's situation than with his own situation."[13] A second theory is from Jack Mezirow's *Transformative Dimensions of Adult Learning*. Mezirow reports the findings of another scholar that "transformations as a response to marginality occurred more frequently in early adult life,"[14] suggesting that such theories of transformation may be especially applicable to a program aimed at traditional undergraduates in a nontraditional educational setting that exposes them to marginality. I want to argue that Hoffman's ideas about the significance of "guilt over affluence" as a highly developed form of empathy dovetail nicely with Moshman's observations about the extraordinary factors that contribute to the disequilibration of conventional moral rationality, with Kennedy's and Evans' educational agenda, and with the first several of Mezirow's ten phases of perspective transformation. These theoretical perspectives, that is, provide something of a hypothesis to be tested against the data of the students' experiences and reflections on them.

One of the most prevalent themes in the data is the students' expression of guilt. It comes up forcefully, for example, when the students learned that the average annual income in the DR was, as reported at that time, just a little more than $1,000. That was precisely the amount that they were advised to bring as *spending* money. Despite their good intentions to help the Dominican poor through their volunteer service, the students discovered early in the semester that they were complicit in the world's inequalities. There are plentiful instances in the data of variations on this theme: Why should I have so much, which I have taken for granted and have not earned, while my Dominican friends, who welcome me into their homes and lives with such generous hospitality, have so little, for which they struggle so hard? Here is a particularly eloquent statement of this theme, worth quoting at some length:

> What I expected to learn from these people is that humanness is a horrible sentence that has been handed down from God, however, I never seem to get what I expect in this place. But what other lesson could I possibly expect to learn down here, especially when I think back to my life in the United States. There I have my own car and live in a nice house with my parents, yet still I look at nicer cars and bigger houses with envy. I could probably fill one closet with clothes that I have and actually wear, and then another one with clothes that haven't seen the light of day in at least a year and I actually complain about having nothing to wear. I have a computer, a television, a phone, a walkman, a diskman, a burner, a stereo, and countless other things to play with but continue to want more toys. I go on exciting trips at least once a year, but still feel like my life is boring. I have enough to eat everyday, but am picky about what I'll put into my mouth. I was given the opportunity to go to great schools to get an education, yet hate it when I have to study. This list could go on forever. I have everything and more than I could ever need, yet still I hate my

> life sometimes. I can not even imagine what it would be like to lack not only all of the extra perks that I've enjoyed in my life, but also some of the necessities. Yet, this is the kind of life that the children in Hogar Luby and my family and friends in Cien Fuegos [a *barrio* filled with people who are living in some of the poorest conditions in the city] live. When I think of how unhappy I am at times in my nothing-for-want life, I don't know how one would deal with a life full of needs and suffering.

Hoffman observes that such a "combination of empathic distress and the mental representation of the plight of an unfortunate group would seem to be the most advanced form of empathic distress."[15] In the case of *Semestre Dominicano*, the opportunities for such distress and representation were intentionally ubiquitous and constant.

Here's how the student just quoted recounts the plight of one of the children she has gotten to know:

> Donald is one of the children that attend the kids kitchen that I've spent some time at in Cien Fuegos. His father passed away from complications due to AIDS not very long ago, and his mother is HIV positive. Because both of his parents have AIDS, chances are good that Donald does too, but his family has never been able to afford to test him. Donald attends the kids kitchen because his mother spends her days working at [a factory in] the Zona Franca [free trade zone], but most of the money that she makes has to go to pay for the little bit of medical attention that she can afford simply to control the pain of her disease. Little is left for Donald, which is another reason he attends the kitchen. It makes it possible for Donald to eat at least one fully nutritious meal a day. Who knows what he gets after he leaves the kitchen? The tough life that Donald has been given shows in the way he interacts with the other kids. Often times he's withdrawn and quiet. It seems as though he is suffering the loss of his father and his childhood. When he's not withdrawn, he is violent and aggressive with the other children, acting out all of the anger that has built up inside of him during his short, but already painful life.

Another student provides the following "representation of the plight of an unfortunate group":

> The realities of the *campos* are very sad right now. The price of coffee is down, and on top of this, there is a very serious blight call *broca* that is eating away at the plants. Both of these have serious repercussions for a community that is built on the cultivation and sale of the crop. This lack of coffee and the sale of coffee have produced a complete lack of other things like money, food, clothes, and proper medical care.

The contrast between their own affluence and the poverty of their new Dominican friends and neighbors induces guilt in the students. Guilt, of course, is usually associated with a loss of self-esteem resulting from recognition of harm done to another. But these students had done no direct harm to any Dominican. They had no hand in constructing the systems of historical and global inequality that they were beginning to recognize benefited and harmed different populations disproportionately. That is why Hoffman calls this "guilt over affluence" a variation of "virtual guilt," which occurs when the individual thinks he is guilty for a harmful act but in fact is not.

As Hoffman notes, "a person may come to believe that by . . . benefiting from privileges others lack, one is responsible for harming others."[16] And this may be perceived as a matter not just of misfortune but of injustice. Hoffman argues that

> . . . a bystander may respond empathetically to someone who needs food and shelter. . . . His empathic distress may also reflect a "caring" principle (we should help those in need). . . . But if he views food and shelter as everyone's "right," then his empathic distress may be transformed in part into a need-based justice response: The victim *deserves* food and shelter. The bystander then not only has empathic feeling for the victim's personal distress but also sees him or her as a victim of injustice whose rights have been violated.[17]

Although adults may experience it, Hoffman classifies guilt over affluence as "*developmental* guilt because it seems more prevalent in adolescents . . . and may be a significant part of the prosocial moral development of those who experience it."[18]

This developmental potential is unleashed especially "if the victim is viewed as basically good," in Hoffman's words, as my students assuredly did. For example, the student who described "the realities of the *campo*" went on to say that "the people are poor, but you might never know it. Instead of trying to bring each other down in order to 'succeed,' they have rallied around each other. They share what little they have and help each other in their work." Such recognition of the essential human goodness of the Dominican poor that these students got to know may, in Hoffman's analysis, transform "empathic distress into an empathic feeling of injustice, including a motive to right the wrong."[19]

After Good Intentions

As their comments in all forms of my documentation indicate, the students came to the DR with a strong motive to serve and to help the poor. As one student wrote, "I came down to the Dominican Republic with grand ideas of service. I was making this big sacrifice, leaving my family, friends and [my boyfriend] for four months so I could make huge differences in people's lives." But actual encounter with impoverished but hospitable Dominicans, coupled with a growing awareness of how little the students could actually do to improve their lives, given their own relative lack of experience, skills, resources, and time, intensified the personal crises brought on by the radically new environment of the first few weeks. But, as this same student remarked, "[I]f service is what I thought it was, then I have been a complete and total failure. . . . I was naïve and patronizing. . . . I, the white, privileged American, was going to make everything better, but I've found out that I have been of little service in comparison with what people have done for me." Or, as another student observed: "What I did not expect was for my view of reality to be changed."

The nadir of this downward emotional trajectory was precipitated by the assigned reading of Ivan Illich's famous speech to North American volunteers in Mexico in 1968. Provocatively titled "To Hell with Good Intentions,"[20] Illich's "piercing words," as one student called them, devastated the *Semestre Dominicano* students. Good intentions, they had discovered by this time, were really all they had to offer, and now they were being told that their good intentions were not welcome, were even part of the problem. As one student put it, "[I]t's taken many hours of being uncomfortable and feeling helpless—sitting there thinking that nothing I can do is going to make a difference, knowing that things cannot remain the way they are, but not knowing what to do or what to think—for me to even start to realize this."

Significantly, however, this student confessed that as much as she had learned from reading Illich, she had learned even more from an honest conversation with her *campo* "dad," the father of the rural family with whom she stayed.

> It both shocked and hurt me [she writes,] when [my dad] sat me down the last night we were in [the *campo*] . . . and told me about some of the consequences of having the Americans come to the *campo*. He told me of the futility of some of our service projects. . . . He told me of the shoddy work that was done on other projects. . . . He also told me that the money spent on some projects could have been better used for other things than what it was used for.

She comes to a painful realization: "It hurt me to think that I might be doing more harm to these people than good. . . . I was not the good person I wanted to consider myself to be." Nonetheless, this student writes that

> I love them [her Dominican friends and family] even though it hurts. It hurts to be compassionate, to empathize with the situations that Dominicans and Haitians alike have to live in. It hurts knowing that I cannot fix everything for them. I suffer knowing of all the injustices and hardships these people face. It would be so much easier not to care. Then I wouldn't cry. . . . I have cried countless tears over the loss of my perfect images of myself and my country. I have mourned the loss of my ignorance, but I know I could never go back to it.

Walter Brueggemann, in an article on education in the Bible, argues that the first "particular practice of passion" to be taught in ancient Israel

> *equips people to cry*, to feel pain, to articulate the anguish, to sense the pathos and act on it. Israel's life with Yahweh begins with a cry (Exodus 2:23–24). That cry is not a confident address to God. Indeed, it is not even addressed to God. Israel's faith does not begin with theological boldness but with social need and social rage. The cry is a desperate assertion that life in its oppressive mode has become unbearable. Such a cry is not only an act of sensitivity but also an act of enormous boldness, for it dramatically delegitimates the claims of the Egyptian empire and announces that the imperial system is dysfunctional and therefore rejected.[21]

It may also seem bold to suggest that learning to cry, to feel pain—the pain of others—and to articulate the anguish should be an educational goal and practice, but that is the claim made here (and throughout this book). The particular anguish articulated by the students of *Semestre Dominicano* deserves a deeper examination.

Moral Anguish as a Disorienting Dilemma

Before leaving for the DR, a colleague had advised me to be on the lookout for what she called "moral distress" in the students. I reported to her after my second round of interviews, just after the encounter with the Illich speech, that what I was observing in my students was better described as "moral anguish." In those interviews, it was not unusual for students to break down and weep when trying to speak of this powerful disillusionment. The "honeymoon period" was emphatically over. Dominicans were still generous and hospitable, but their poverty—now seen as deprivation causing unjust suffering—was no longer romanticized. The vibrant, sun-drenched, and music-saturated island culture was still alluring, but its injustice, suffering, and misery were also acknowledged and critiqued.

There was at this point the danger of what Hoffman calls "empathic over-arousal," which "can move observers out of the empathic mode, cause them to be preoccupied with their own personal distress, and turn their attention away from the victim."[22] But by the end of the semester, it was clear that the students as a group had moved past any over-arousal to the challenge of the inexorable transition back home. Over and over one hears in their interviews, journals, and papers, both their anxiety that they might forget what they had learned in the DR and their determination not to. As one student wrote, "[T]he children at Hogar Luby and my friends and family at Cien Fuegos have in fact become my heroes, my role models, and my inspiration, and they will remain in my heart forever. I just hope that I will never forget all that they have taught me ['the secret to our lives as humans'] because it would be a disservice to them, to this program, and, most of all, to myself."

Few had concrete ideas how they were going to make a difference appropriate to what they had learned, to their new perspective, but all were committed to find ways to do so. As one student wrote in a final paper, "[T]his experience has changed my goals and visions for my future. Before, I wanted a nice paying and somewhat prestigious job. Now these things are much less important to me. I have realized that I do not need all the material things that I wanted for myself before. The people I have met here that live simply are the kind of people I want to be like. They know what life is all about. They do not let greed interfere with love."

Hoffman observes that "an emotionally powerful 'triggering event'" such as "extreme injustice" may cause one "to reexamine one's life choices" and may lead "to a new moral perspective and sense of social responsibility."[23] More particularly, Hoffman suggests there are "two necessary conditions" for guilt over affluence to become such a triggering event: "(a) direct exposure to the less fortunate whose lives can then be vividly imagined, . . . and (b) cultural nonjustification for vast discrepancies in wealth."[24] What Hoffman calls a "triggering event" in the process of moral perspective transformation, what Moshman addresses as "disequilibration," and what appears in various guises in Kennedy's and Evans' educational programs, Mezirow calls a "disorienting dilemma," the first of ten phases identified in his process of perspective transformation, the first four of which I have demonstrated were substantively and effectively present in *Semestre Dominicano*:

1. A disorienting dilemma
2. Self-examination with feelings of guilt or shame

3. Critical assessment of epistemic, sociocultural, or psychic assumptions
4. Recognition that one's discontent and the process of transformation are shared and that others have negotiated a similar change

Phases 5 and 6 can be seen only in the most initial of ways:

5. Exploration of options for new roles, relationships, and actions
6. Planning of a course of action

Finally, phases 7–10 are matters of longer term vocational discernment and preparation:

7. Acquisition of knowledge and skills for implementing one's plans
8. Provisional trying of new roles
9. Building of competence and self-confidence in new roles and relationships
10. Reintegration into one's life on the basis of conditions dictated by one's new perspective[25]

Conclusion: Empathy and Commitment to Social Change

In *Inventing Human Rights: A History*, Lynn Hunt argues that in eighteenth-century Europe, "reading accounts of torture or epistolary novels [such a Samuel Richardson's *Pamela* or *Clarissa* or Rousseau's *Julie*] had physical effects that translated into brain changes and came back as new concepts about the organization of social and political life. New kinds of reading (and viewing and listening) created new individual experiences (empathy), which in turn made possible new social and political concepts (human rights)." Or more simply, "for human rights to become self-evident, ordinary people had to have new understandings that came from new kinds of feelings."[26]

Adam Hochschild in *Bury the Chains*, his narrative of the movement to abolish slavery in late eighteenth- and early nineteenth-century England, suggests that the methods of the 12 men who initiated abolitionism indicate that they "placed their hope not in [the authority of] sacred texts, but in human empathy."[27] And they were astonishingly successful, as the first grass-roots human rights movement in history, within their own lifetimes. Their first meeting was held in 1787.[28] Slavery was abolished, and nearly 800,000 slaves were emancipated in the British Empire in 1838.[29]

More recently if in less-dramatic circumstances, Daloz, Keen, Keen, and Parks, in *Common Fire*,[30] their study of "more than one hundred people who had sustained long-term commitments to work on behalf of the common good,"[31] report that "the single most important pattern we have found . . . is what we have come to call *a constructive, enlarging engagement with the other* [italics in original]. It is the primary dynamic that . . . appeared at some point during the formation of the commitment of *everyone in our sample*" [emphasis added].[32] In such encounters, writes Sharon Parks in her book *Big Questions, Worthy Dreams*[33] as she reflects on the findings she helped produce as a co-author of *Common Fire*, "an empathic bond arises from recognizing that the other suffers in the same way as we, having the same capacity for hope, longing, love, joy, and pain." Furthermore, "this kind of perspective taking gives rise to compassion. . . . [which] in turn gives rise to a conviction of possibility, the sense that there has to be a better way." And most importantly, echoing the developmental insight reported by Martin Hoffman, "young adulthood is a time of special readiness for this expansion of soul."[34]

Research on *Semestre Dominicano* suggests that such an educational program, with its emphasis on personal encounter with the poor as a problem-posing *insertion* into social reality (as well as the other dimensions of the Pedagogical Circle), and with the human capacity for empathy at its heart, provides one very promising model by which to foster in college students a transformation of moral perspective and a commitment to a more-just world. That such a transformation is oftentimes painful has been a theme of this chapter (as it will be of the following chapter). But as psychologist John Sanford has observed, "'truly great people have never had much peace of mind, for they were too aware of their inner conflicts, of the pain and suffering around them, and of their own calling to a life of struggle.'"[35] Or, to quote a classic work of Walter Brueggemann, "the riddle and insight of biblical faith is the awareness that only anguish leads to life, only grieving leads to joy, and only embraced endings permit new beginnings."[36]

Programs such as *Semestre Dominicano* require great commitments of time, energy, and resources from both the participants and the sponsoring institutions. As powerful as they can be, they will inevitably reach only a relatively small number of students. What can be done in a similar vein but more accessibly and affordably for both participants and institutions? That is the subject of the next chapter.

5 "We Make the Road by Stumbling"

Aristotle, Service-Learning, and Justice

I felt shame coming up in my body.

A service-learning student

Introduction: The Pain of Self-Disclosure

In *Pedagogy of Hope*, Paulo Freire relates "the most bruising lesson"[1] he had received in his life as an educator. Early in his career, he was giving a talk in Recife, in the extremely impoverished northeast of Brazil, on Jean Piaget's *The Moral Judgment of the Child*.[2] At the conclusion, "a man of about forty, still rather young, but already worn out and exhausted, . . . raised his hand and gave a talk that [the famous educator has] never been able to forget." He reports, many years later, that this peasant's remarks "seared my soul for good and all." What could a poor and uneducated man say that would make such a lifelong difference to this representative of the university-trained elite?

First, he described in detail the living circumstances of people like himself. He spoke of "their pitiful houses, . . . the lack of facilities, . . . the lack of resources for the most basic necessities. He spoke of physical exhaustion, and of the impossibility of dreams for a better tomorrow." Freire began to slouch into his chair. Then the man described Freire's house, although he had never seen it. It was not cramped by other houses and even had a yard. A bedroom for the parents, another for the daughters, and yet another for the sons. A bathroom with running water. A kitchen with appliances. A maid's room. The good professor surely had a study or library for the many books he had read. Freire, "scrunching further down into [his] chair," had to acknowledge that in his interlocutor's portrait of his world, spacious and comfortable, "there was nothing to add or subtract."

The probably illiterate peasant had pinned the bookish professor like a bug in a museum case. True to form as a man of letters, Freire remarks that "the discourse of that faraway night is still before me, as if it had been a written text, an essay I constantly had to review." This collision of the worlds of rich and poor, comfortable and afflicted, literate and illiterate, was the culmination of Freire's own learning process as a progressive educator.[3]

For some of us, our most crucial learning comes burdened with the pain of self-disclosure.

Conceptual and Research Background

The research for this chapter began as a review of the literature on service-learning and justice in university settings, with special attention to investigations of student outcomes. My hope was to identify the most successful courses and programs and to articulate a kind of unified field theory of best practices. Surely that would be useful to progressive educators in the United States, so many of them inspired by Paulo Freire, who himself took inspiration from John Dewey,[4] often described as a principal philosophical source for service-learning pedagogy.[5] So the one article of the more than 60 I reviewed that especially caught my eye cited neither Dewey nor Freire as progenitors of service-learning, but rather Aristotle, referred to by Icelandic scholar Kristján Kristjánsson as "the grandfather of service learning."[6] I had just published an article on "Aristotle for Contemporary Moral Educators,"[7] but had not thought to explicate the author of the *Nicomachean Ethics* as a theoretical resource for service-learning.

The second thing that caught my eye was the frequency with which investigations of service-learning outcomes reported student experiences not unlike that of Paulo Freire in Recife. In almost one-third of the articles or chapters reviewed, students were cited as having painful or distressing emotions. It seemed, in fact, that the closer the report hewed to individual student experiences, the more likely it was that such feelings had been articulated in the context of the service-learning course or program. A line from an unremembered poet came to mind: "scars make your body more interesting." Maybe emotional bruises make your service-learning experience more meaningful, as did that encounter in Recife for Freire, when he couldn't hide from the truth of his privilege as spotlighted by one of the presumed recipients of his educational *noblesse oblige*. In this case, the oppressed educated the educator. Perhaps in justice education, we make the road not only by walking[8] but also, at least sometimes, by stumbling, by losing our emotional footing, our psychological balance.

As I ruminated on this pattern of emotional upheaval in the service-learning and justice literature, doing so in intellectual proximity to that somewhat surprising article on service-learning and Aristotle, I remembered another article on Aristotle and moral education from my earlier research project: It was provocatively titled "Aristotle's Painful Path to Virtue," by Howard J. Curzer.[9] Might there be an even deeper relationship between service-learning, at least service-learning for justice, and moral formation in an Aristotelian mode? Might the sociomoral aims of service-learning go beyond not only the fostering of charitable impulses toward the less privileged, but also beyond a heightened sense of civic responsibility, beyond more active participation in democratic life, even beyond a greater commitment to social justice?[10] Dare service-learning practitioners aim at the development of the *virtue* of justice in our students? It is the purpose of this chapter to make the case that however educators with a focus on justice articulate their ultimate aims as service-learning practitioners, getting there seems to involve sometimes painful disruption of the emotional lives of our students.

This chapter proceeds in four steps. First, I outline Kristjánsson's argument for Aristotle as a theoretical source for service-learning. Second, I present examples of service-learning student outcomes in which painful emotions play a prominent role. Third, I outline Curzer's argument that Aristotle's path to virtue is a sometimes painful one. This completes the conceptual circle: Aristotle and service-learning; service-learning and painful emotions; painful emotions and Aristotle (Figure 5.1). Fourth and last, I reflect briefly on what it might

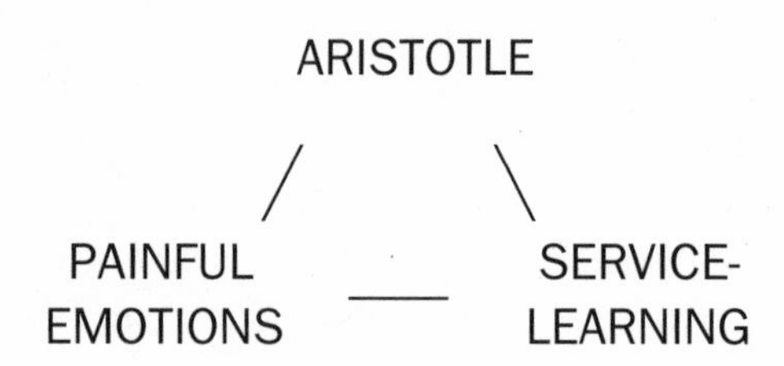

Figure 5.1

mean to disrupt our students' lives through service-learning experiences of injustice in the lives of others.

Aristotle and Service-Learning

Kristjánsson begins with his own painful emotion. He observes that he is "probably not the only moral philosopher whose child has posed the chilling question: 'What have *you* done to help those children?'" (p. 267; emphasis in original).[11] *Those children* are most tragically the 33,000 who die unnecessarily from malnutrition and related diseases every day and whose deaths "could be prevented if every person in the western world who was reasonably well off diverted as little as 2 per cent of their income to famine relief and global population control" (pp. 267–68).[12] Kristjánsson then comments that people like us should be "properly shamed into action by that deceptively simple question raised by our own children" (p. 268). A scholar of Aristotle, Kristjánsson might further have observed that shame is described as a semi- or quasi-virtue in the *Nicomachean Ethics* (IV.9), but only in the young. The fully virtuous adult would never have an occasion to experience shame.

But who among us in a world of 33,000 unnecessary childhood deaths every day could ever do enough *not* to feel some shame when asked such a question? For all its ordinariness, it is nonetheless a painful emotion to the morally sensitive. But Kristjánsson doesn't let us off the hook: "we who look for stomach for our meat while others look for meat for their stomach . . . are simply not being *generous* enough. And generosity is a moral virtue, the lack of which constitutes a moral vice" (p. 268; emphasis in orginal). This issue, then, surely should be "engaged with head-on in moral-education classes" (p. 268) where "the cultivation of a generous personality: personality as a character state (*hexis*) in the Aristotelian sense," would be a "worthy aim" (p. 271).

How is this cultivation to be accomplished? Kristjánsson reminds us of the general process of moral sensitization according to Aristotle: "the virtues are first activated through habituation; then polished through comparisons with others; and, finally, refined through critical assessment and reassessment once the moral learner has acquired practical wisdom (*phronesis*)" (p. 278). Here is the payoff: "The modern method of moral education which comes closest to Aristotle's description . . . is that of service-learning. Through service-learning, the child is exposed to real-world experiences and instructed in acting virtuously in the given circumstances. This is done in the hope that such virtuous actions will become ingrained parts of the child's character" (p. 278). But, Kristjánsson observes, "a service-learning initiative involving the homeless is probably a waste of time . . . unless it is accompanied by the students' critical reflection, guided by their teacher, on such issues as the plight of today's homeless and the growing economic disparity between rich and poor" (p. 279).

It would seem we are moving from generosity strictly considered to social justice broadly understood, but that, according to Kristjánsson, is a very Aristotelian move. For Aristotle, "there is, of course, no . . . distinction to be found between the personal and political: political action is considered to ensue naturally and seamlessly from personal virtues." Not to make this move is to "'do without generosity in order to practice charity.'"[13] That is, personal generosity, private charity, or traditional alms-giving is not the only virtuous action necessary in a world of 33,000 unnecessary childhood deaths each day. If we can be properly shamed by our piddling generosity, we can also be pained by a lack of *action for justice* within the polis.

Service-Learning and Painful Emotions

What Aristotle calls the semi-virtue of shame is just one of the painful emotions that might come our way when, perhaps in a service-learning experience, we are made to acknowledge our complicity in a world of needless suffering and social injustice. What follows is a review of the findings of four studies of service-learning relevant to our theme.

"A shocking experience"

Kerry Ann Rockquemore and Regan Harwell Schaeffer[14] asked 50 students participating in service-learning courses at Pepperdine University to keep journals responding to five questions, including "How did my service make me feel today?" The purpose of this question was to create qualitative data reflective of the students' "emotional reactions to the events they encountered in their placement agencies." Pepperdine students are reported to be more racially homogeneous (80% white) and higher in parental socioeconomic status (the majority had family incomes of at least $75,000 and one-fourth of at least $150,000) than the general population of college students. Their service-learning courses involved them in "food delivery, residential geriatric care, youth mentoring, public education, juvenile detention, free health services, free legal aid, shelter for the homeless, and after-school mentoring" (p. 15).

The authors report that these relatively privileged students described their first close encounter with poverty as "a shocking experience." Drawing out the metaphor and the significance of the experience, the authors observe that "the shock stage of service-learning is important because it provides a sharp emotional and psychological jolt to students' perceptions of reality" (p. 16). More particularly,

> [E]xperiencing other people living in poverty, students were forced to open themselves up to the realization that their perceptions of the social world may be severely skewed by their affluence and/or Christian worldview. This shock-induced uncertainty, while frightening and upsetting to some students, created in them an ideal state of cognitive openness

> toward the substantive course material. This stage of shock enabled students to examine the inconsistencies in their lives and in the community around them. (p. 17)

This self-examination is reported to have caused students to make "significant changes in their *attitudes* toward social justice, equality of opportunity, and civic responsibility over the course of the semester" (p. 15; emphasis added). However, if one is shocked or even frightened into heightened social awareness, one may also be angered into new kinds of social action.

"I feel the anger"

Lee Artz[15] describes his course "Critical Ethnography for Communications Studies" as an attempt to move from a focus on charity to a focus on social justice in service-learning. Drawing on Antonio Gramsci's theory of hegemony and Paulo Freire's dialogic *praxis*, Artz encourages his students toward an examination of cultural and structural factors in the experience of those "served"—the marginalized. He hopes to foster solidarity between his students and the subordinate communities with whom they enter into relationship. In his own words, "the ambitious objective of this service-learning course is for students to engage in dialogue, reflection, and action with other participants in social struggle and—using their knowledge of communication theories and their skills in communication practices—to help implement communication strategies and tactics for overcoming the conditions confronted as unjust" (p. 245).

The few times when Artz reports directly on the students' experience, anger on behalf of those in the marginalized communities who are now known personally emerges as a theme. One student took issue with the very concept of service as applied to his participation: "'I'm not there for service. I'm part of this. There isn't that power differential, that patronizing attitude that comes with 'helping' someone. I feel the anger'" (p. 247). Another student-participant so identified with the community that "she was angered by a group of Junior League women who treated the homeless women to an occasional 'night out' bowling with the girls. She felt a real discomfort listening to the volunteers commiserate over their affluent lifestyle problems in light of the struggles of the homeless women" (p. 248). This incipient solidarity with the marginalized influenced the same student's vocational discernment: "I thought about the choices I have as a communication major. I could choose to be in the corporate sphere . . . or I could be employed in social justice" (p. 248). The author reports that this student continued to work with the homeless women and decided on a social justice concentration in her major. The painful emotion of anger may be part of the process of change when service-learning courses allow students to develop meaningful relationships with those disparaged by mainstream society.

"Rattled to the bone"

Michelle Dunlap, Jennifer Scoggin, Patrick Green, and Angelique Davi[16] provide a sophisticated model of how 13 relatively affluent service-learning students dealt with a growing awareness of their own white privilege and of the socioeconomic disparity between themselves and the people of color they encounter in their service. Progress through the model's five stages (Trigger Event, Grappling, Personalization, Divided Self, and Disequilibrium Resolution) hinges on the distinction between assimilation and accommodation, between appropriating new information into one's current worldview or changing one's worldview to make room for new information. The Trigger Event is "usually one in which the student is confronted with another's circumstance involving a great deal of disadvantage, making the former's privilege even more apparent" and resulting in "discomfort or confusion" (p. 20).

One student who had experienced such a confrontation reported being "'rattled to the bone'" and that he felt "'a chill down [his] spine. As if you were watching a movie with extremely depressing parts. This was not a movie; these were real people, with real problems'" (p. 21). Another student, identified as in the Grappling stage ("they begin to understand and search for explanations for the socioeconomic inequities, institutional racism, and systems of privilege in place in our country"), wrote in her journal that "after starting the service work I realized how angry at the world I was. . . . It just makes me mad that I have to wake up everyday in a world that is so disrespectful to people" (p. 22). Another student wrote that she "felt angry that our country, which is one of the wealthiest and most powerful in the world, could allow this epidemic of homelessness to occur." In such reflections, observe the authors, "the students are expressing disequilibrium or dissonance between what they thought they knew and what they are finding to be true, and their emotional reactions to that dissonance."

In addition to anger, the painful emotions in these early stages may include sadness, pity, guilt, discomfort, shock, fear, and anxiety (p. 23). In stage 4, Divided Self, guilt especially may be present as students experience themselves as torn between what they thought they knew (their intellectual knowledge) and the new experiential knowledge of the victims' perspective that they have acquired as a result of their service-learning encounters and relationships (p. 24–25). Such an experience of self-division or self-conflict may be a powerful opportunity for new self-knowledge.

"A bad feeling in my stomach"

James Ostrow[17] provides a fine-grained social-phenomenological investigation (heavily indebted to the theory of Irving Goffman) of the self-consciousness of white affluent students from a business college as they visit a homeless shelter:

> . . . [I]t is through their self-consciousness that students are confronted with their own economic and cultural positioning as a distancing force between themselves and the guests [of the shelter]. As they become alert to these extrapersonal grounds of their relations with the guests, students are compelled to revise their stated opinions about what the homeless individuals are "really like." (p. 358)

More importantly, however, is the revision of previously *un*stated opinions about themselves. Visiting the homeless shelter, the students participate in "the process of being acutely aware of what we are taken *as* in the eyes of the beholders within the context of remembered, anticipated, or actual encounters. . . . We are rendered problematic for ourselves *as what we are* . . ." (p. 359; emphasis in original).

Ostrow's observations about the students' experiences are based on "791 journals or sets of field notes collected over a four and one-half year period" (p. 359). I simply highlight a few of the students' own writings of the many that Ostrow reports. After a conversation with a homeless woman, one student wrote that, "'If anyone was humbled from this experience, it was me'" (p. 361). Another student was left speechless by a homeless man's. life-story and writes that, "'Before I could attempt to break the uncomfortable silence, he told me never to forget how lucky I was and to never turn my back on those in need. He got up and left me sitting in shock'" (p. 361). Besides being humbled or shocked, Ostrow observes that "these sorts of experiences also induce expressions of anger, through which many students assert their views or changes in view" (p. 362).

Likewise, "fear is a part of the students' hyperattentiveness" to their new surroundings, particularly in regard to "what their own presence will mean for the inhabitants." Students experience themselves as "strangers impressing themselves into a setting with which others are all too familiar" (p. 364). One student reported feeling "'as though we were exhibits at a zoo and the adults were watching us. I thought it would be the other way around, but it wasn't.'" Ostrow writes that "students often suggest that they are virtual walking magnets of resentment." One homeless woman made it clear to a student "'that she understood I was there because I had to be here not because I wanted to be. She [the homeless woman] felt like a 'rat in a laboratory experiment' as she put it. I tried to explain to her that it was not true but in a way it was. I felt so bad and ashamed of myself. . . . '" Another student wrote that "'I seemed to feel as if their impression of us was that we were just spoiled little college brats doing charity work,'" while yet another "'was afraid that they were seeing me as a spoiled rich kid'" (p. 366).

Through such experiences, writes Ostrow (quoting Sartre), students become "'luminous to themselves' . . . as alien presences, as disturbances in a world that is not their own" (p. 369). The experience is often accompanied by emotional pain. As one student wrote in a compellingly visceral reflection: "I had a bad feeling in my stomach because I was remembering how well I ate at lunch . . . seeing people rush to table for food, I felt shame coming up in my body. . . ." (p. 373). One is reminded of Kristjánsson's description of such encounters between rich and poor as between those "who look for stomach for our meat while others look for meat for their stomach." It is as if that last student quoted were vomiting up his previously unacknowledged privilege, laying it out on the table for all to see. Or, as Ostrow himself observes, "it is as though what the students are habitually becomes their own worst enemy" (p. 374). That may be a viscerally painful experience, indeed, but one that perhaps puts these young people more determinedly on the painful path to virtue.

But what do such experiences of being humbled, shocked, angered, frightened, and ashamed have to so with moral education in Aristotelian mode?

The Painful Path to Virtue

Howard Curzer's article, "Aristotle's Painful Path to Virtue,"[18] provides a critique of, and an alternative to, Myles Burnyeat's classic essay, "Aristotle on Learning to Be Good" (1980). Curzer summarizes Burnyeat's interpretation thusly:

> (A) Aristotle thinks that the learner is given virtue judgments about particular acts in particular situations. (B) The learner internalizes these judgments by habitual virtuous action. (C) This guided habituation also yields the ability to identify virtuous acts. (D) The learner is motivated to perform virtuous acts again and again by taking pleasure in them. (E) Conversely, the learner comes to take proper pleasure in virtuous acts by performing them. (p. 144)

The problem with what Curzer calls this "common sense" view of moral development is that it overstates the role Aristotle himself attributes to pleasure in the acquisition of virtue. Indeed, "Aristotle is actually committed to the view that *learners do not typically enjoy virtuous acts at all*" (p. 149; emphasis in original). According to Aristotle, "'One cannot get the pleasures of a just man without being just'. . . . So [Curzer infers that] learners do not learn that virtuous acts are pleasant by performing and enjoying them, because learners do not enjoy them. Indeed virtuous action is painful for learners" (p. 149). "If," as Aristotle asserts, "virtue acquisition is like craft acquisition, perhaps learning to act virtuously is also a painful process. . . . [Indeed,] virtuous acts are *not* typically overall pleasant *even for the virtuous*, let alone for learners" (p. 150; emphasis in original).

We might not take *unmitigated* pleasure in parting with that minimal two percent of our affluence that Kristjánsson recommends as an expression of our concern for hungry children. Even to achieve an overall pleasure in the act, and not the higher standard of unmitigated pleasure, the act must achieve its proper end (p.152). In the case of eliminating the unnecessary deaths of 33,000 children daily, what are the chances of that? In other words, "virtuous action is often impeded. And impeded virtuous action is not overall pleasant" (p. 153).

Of course, the most intimate impediment to virtuous action is our own lack of virtue. Indeed, many of us "come to perform virtuous acts from fear of the painful feeling we might call shame, guilt, or remorse. . . . People who feel *aidōs* [shame] for not doing certain things, for not living a certain way believe that they should do these things, should live this way. This is a belief about intrinsic value and thus about ultimate ends. It begets a desire to lead a certain type of life" (p. 159). On Curzer's interpretation, over against Burnyeat's, "pain rather than pleasure drives moral development. . . . Although this darker view is less comforting, it is more plausible and more consistent with Aristotle's text" (p. 162).

This darker view of moral development is also more consistent with the most compelling investigations of student outcomes, as reported in their own words, in their own journals, in service-learning courses and programs with a focus on social justice. It is a paradox of this dark process of moral sensitization that students could become "luminous to themselves." That paradox, I believe, is what Aristotle called, strangely, the "semi-virtue" of shame. Those other painful emotions mentioned earlier—being humbled, shocked, angered, and so on—would seem simply to come with the territory defined most characteristically by the experience of shame when the affluent student encounters the homeless, when the progressive educator meets the clear-eyed peasant, when the moral philosopher is questioned by his own child.

Disrupting Our Students' Lives

Michael Schratz and Rob Walker[19] observe that service-learning may "disrupt" the lives of students; that in service-learning, students learn most about themselves; that service-learning occasions the rebuilding of the participants' own lives and senses of self; and that "critical incidents" such as those that occur in service-learning may have deep impact on learning, and that such incidents are often connected with loss. Service-learning at its best and deepest is about the disruption and loss that is a first step or prerequisite to the transformation of self. Service-learning instructors invite their students into a potentially uncomfortable and even painful personal process. Such an invitation presumes that whatever selves students bring to class, they are in some sense inadequate or in need of development, expansion, redefinition.

This presumption may seem, well, presumptuous, judgmental, and even arrogant. It is at the opposite end of the pedagogical spectrum from a so-called "values-free" imparting of impersonal knowledge or proficiency. Who are we to make such a judgment about our students? What is the norm or standard by which we can make such a judgment *justifiably*? What large and seemingly nonacademic roles and responsibilities does it assume on the part of the teacher in relation to the student? What kind of structures and opportunities of care and attention are provided so that this process of personal deconstruction and reconstruction can take place humanely and effectively? The issue, it seems to me, is not so much to minimize the risk but rather to maximize the potential for growing *through* the risk. Indeed, the more risk, the greater the potential for growth (but also for alienation). Katherine

Kirby makes this point in an essay on her service-learning course, "Courageous Faith and Moral Formation: Trust, Respect, and Self-Confidence." She argues that the six students in the class of 18 who took the path of most emotional resistance by choosing to serve in a nursing home for seniors rather than a school for refugee children "had the most transformative experiences" precisely "because the moral formation accomplished by these students required a greater amount of what [she] would call 'courageous faith.'"[20]

On the other hand, although it may seem arrogant for faculty, from a position of authority and power, to presume to invite students into a process of self-transformation toward a normative ideal of the human person, it also means for the faculty, paradoxically, a loss of control seldom experienced in a traditional lecture environment and a necessary admission of relative if not complete incompetence—for who among us is trained to deal with young adults in the grip of doubt and anxiety about their very selves? Although service-learning as a transformative pedagogy may seem arrogant on the part of the teacher, in fact, it calls for a deep humility and even reverence toward the students' experience, which is not subject to faculty control (or indifference) as in the traditional lecture hall.

In a Catholic university, we do have a standard or norm or ideal to orient and justify service-learning and the real risks that it entails for us and our students. That standard has been encapsulated as a "well-educated solidarity with the real world."[21] This implies not only a normative vision of education but even more controversially in a secularized, pluralistic culture, a normative vision of the human person. The well-educated person is not only intellectually and professionally competent but also just, caring, compassionate, discerning, committed, and faithful in a real world characterized by gross injustice and widespread suffering.

The invitation to transformation that is implicit in service-learning with a focus on justice calls for a certain trust on the part of the teacher that the dynamics of human nature, as understood by Aristotle, do indeed include the capacity of the self to grow through disruption and even psychic, moral, and spiritual distress toward a more discerning, expansive, and vital self and relationship to the "real world." Service-learning in this perspective, at this level, and even within secular institutions (as were most of the schools from which the student outcomes reported above were drawn), is in itself profession of at least a humanistic faith. When service-learning is well integrated into the curricula of Catholic universities it is, of course, much more than that. Within the Pedagogical Circle, such insertion into social reality must be accompanied not only by social analysis, as Kristjánsson recommends, but also by theological and normative reflection, and by vocational discernment.

The chilling question that Professor Kristjánsson's child put to him—"What have *you* done to help those children?"—is not unlike the questions central to the vision of the last judgment of Matthew 25:31–46: "'Lord, when did we see you hungry and feed you, or thirsty and give you drink? When did we see you a stranger and welcome you, or naked and clothe you? When did we see you ill or in prison, and visit you?' And the king will say to them in reply, 'Amen, I say to you, whatever you did for one of these least brothers of mine, you did to me.'" Catholic social teaching reminds us over and over again that such imperatives demand not only acts of personal compassion and almsgiving but also solidarity and commitment to social justice. Well-done service-learning, as an expression of the Pedagogical Circle, is a powerful way to prepare students to "meet their maker" at the Last Judgment by meeting him now in homeless shelters and soup kitchens, detention centers and inner-city classrooms. Such experiences may lead students to declare, as did Paulo Freire after his encounter with an illiterate but articulate peasant, it "seared my soul for good and all."

The reader's imaginative engagement with this scene from Freire's life, as recorded in one of his books, suggests a third justice pedagogy: one that complements but also depends upon service-learning courses or immersion programs to provide students with their own searing personal encounters. But the study of extraordinary figures like Paulo Freire, in both their achievements and their struggles, can be accomplished without leaving the classroom. The teaching of moral exemplars such as Dorothy Day, Rev. Martin Luther King, Jr., and Archbishop Oscar Romero as a justice pedagogy is the subject of the following chapter.

6 Meetings with Remarkable Men and Women

On Teaching Moral Exemplars

> For us men there are only two possibilities in this world: either we become ever better or ever worse; there is simply no such thing as standing still.
>
> *Franz Jägerstätter*[1]

The Course, the Pedagogy

Since the first offering in the fall of 1995, I have taught some 50 sections of an upper-division undergraduate seminar titled "Faith and Moral Development," a required course in the Justice and Peace Studies Program, which I direct. The course is innovative or at least unusual in three ways. First, it is structured as a sequence of three one-credit sections taken over the span of three semesters. The basic rationale for this structure is that such continuity of participation provides a better opportunity for building a sense of intellectual community than if students took a conventional three-credit course for only one semester. Second, one of the major requirements of the syllabus is that the students themselves take turns leading the weekly discussions. This also contributes to the classroom community as students take personal ownership for the presentation of material, on which the quality of the sessions largely depends.

The third noteworthy dimension of the seminar, which I reflect on more fully in this chapter, is its subject matter. We study personal exemplars of faith and moral development and various theoretical perspectives on that development. The pedagogical format of each section is the same, but the content, the assigned texts—the exemplars themselves—are different from section to section and from semester to semester (although there is some repetition from year to year). A growing research literature on moral exemplars themselves does exist, but I have discovered sparse research on the teaching of moral exemplars as a method of moral education. Thus, if I am to achieve any conceptual clarity on this particular moral pedagogy, which my own experience suggests is rich in possibilities, I must come at it from a variety of sources other than current research on the topic itself.

Alasdair MacIntyre's writings on the necessity of a determinate human *telos* (end or goal) within local traditions of moral practice and inquiry seem to provide a philosophical justification for a course such as the one this chapter is exploring (see Chapter 3). Aristotle, MacIntyre's own principal source, provides some tantalizingly relevant comments on emulation and youthful character in his *Rhetoric*,[2] and he will be our principal source also in this chapter. This consideration of youthful character suggests that the concept of liminality may serve as a prism through which to view several dimensions of the young adult college experience. The vast literature on religious saints, described by John Coleman as "liminal figures who both belong and do not quite belong to ordinarily structured social reality,"[3] includes perspectives on saints as exemplars that may provide insight into moral exemplars by way of analogy. Nietzsche,[4] from a very different philosophical perspective, offers a surprisingly relevant discussion of the role of exemplars in personal development. Finally, Andrew Michael Flescher,[5] although he does not address pedagogical issues extensively, does analyze in great depth the relation between the extraordinary morality of heroes and saints and the morality of ordinary people, and more importantly outlines "the thesis of moral development," which becomes central to my argument for teaching moral exemplars.

A disclaimer: Let me be clear from the outset that I do not endorse a simple mimetic psychology as charmingly advocated by Charlie Brown in the venerable cartoon strip *Peanuts*. In the first frame, Linus "twangs" a make-believe bow-and-arrow; in the background, Lucy comments to Charlie, "Oh, good grief! Now he's Robin Hood!" In the next two frames Lucy runs through a list of other roles Linus has taken on after seeing various movies: skin diver, cowboy, mountain climber.

Finally Charlie turns to Lucy and asks, "Why don't you take him to a movie about Albert Schweitzer?"

I do not believe that simply by exposing students to a moral exemplar like Albert Schweitzer that they will irresistibly imitate the compassion, commitment, and conviction of the great humanitarian physician, biblical scholar, and musicologist. Human development is not like that, as Charles Schulz, the creator of *Peanuts*, slyly implies. Yet wouldn't Linus's imagination be enriched by seeing an age-appropriate movie about Dr. Schweitzer? And if we can imagine a character from the comics page actually growing up and developing, can't we also imagine him taking a deep personal interest in a critical biography of and analytic perspective on such a person? Can't we imagine Linus as a college student engaging in lively discussion with his peers about a Schweitzer or Gandhi or King and the issues such exemplary lives raise for idealistic young people on the cusp of adulthood?

This chapter is an attempt to elucidate what might be going on in those young minds and hearts as I have listened in on hundreds of such conversations and read thousands of pages of personal reflections and essays over the past 15 years. Before delving into what Aristotle can contribute to this exploration, let's take a quick look at how Alasdair MacIntyre might provide a rationale for such a course.

Alasdair MacIntyre on the Moral Self

Two themes from MacIntyre are especially relevant to the discussion of moral exemplars in justice education. First, for MacIntyre, there can be no coherent personal moral identity or self apart from participation in a tradition of social practices and moral enquiry and apart from narratives that embody that tradition. I believe that the biographies of moral exemplars as taught in my course represent such narratives. Narratives of the lives of Gandhi and King, to cite only two of the most luminous justice exemplars, embody the practice of *satyagraha* (truth-force) in South Africa and India and of militant nonviolence in the U.S. South in the struggle for freedom, justice, and peace, as well as Gandhi's and King's consistent self-reflective inquiry about such practices. Apart from such narratives, how would we know what it means for the individual and a community to embrace nonviolence as a means of social struggle? How would we otherwise be able to identify the virtues required in such struggle? As Flescher observes, "the value of such literature is that it helps us to reframe in our own minds exactly what is 'possible' or 'realistic' in terms of setting standards for our responsibilities to others."[6]

Second, MacIntyre argues not only that "every human being . . . lives out her or his life in a narrative form" but also that such narratives "are structured in terms of a *telos*, of virtues and of rules in an Aristotelian mode."[7] An excerpt from the *Eudemian Ethics*[8] will help to place this emphasis on *telos* in its original Aristotelian context:

> Taking note of these things [the question of what contributes to human happiness], everyone who can live according to his own choice should adopt some goal for the fine life, whether it be honour or reputation or wealth or cultivation—an aim that he will have in view in all his actions; for not to have ordered one's life in relation to some end is a mark of extreme folly. But above all, and before everything else, he should settle in his own mind—neither in a hurried nor in a dilatory manner—in which human thing living well consists, and what those things are without which it [living well] cannot belong to human beings. (1214b)

In Catholic universities today, thanks especially to the many programs funded by Lilly Endowment, Inc. promoting the exploration of vocation (broadly conceived), we are more likely to speak of vocation or calling than of the *telos* or goal of a human life. However, the impetus to see one's life as a whole and as moving intentionally in a discerned direction is the same in either case.

But even without such deliberate reflection and discernment, according to MacIntyre, every human narrative offers an image of the end or purpose or ideal of human life and of what is required to reach it. My own argument would be that the lives of moral exemplars present such images of the human *telos*, of what it means to live a fully human life. Without them, how would we know what is possible for us as human beings? As MacIntyre himself has written, "we learn what kind of quality truthfulness or courage is, what its practice amounts to, what obstacles it creates and what it avoids and so on only in key part by observing its practice in others and in ourselves."[9] I believe this is true not only of specific virtues but of the virtuous life as a whole. The "Faith and Moral Development" seminar engages small communities of students in sustained moral inquiry into the practices and virtues relevant to the pursuit of social justice and peace as they are embodied in the lives of exemplary persons most of whom have themselves thought long and hard about their own *telos* or vocation.

Aristotle on Emulation in the Young

In the *Nicomachean Ethics*, Aristotle puts the wise person, his equivalent of the moral exemplar, at the heart of his definition of *arête*: "Virtue [excellence], then, is a state [disposition], consisting in a mean, the mean relative to us, which is defined [determined] by reference to reason, that is to say, to the reason by reference to which the prudent [wise] person would define it" [1107a].[10] What saves this definition from apparent circularity is its context in the received moral traditions of the *polis* (the organized community), which achieve their fulfillment in the lives of *phronimoi* (wise persons, or moral exemplars). We look to the best among us to understand what it means to be fully human: to achieve our *telos*, our end or purpose, according to our own tradition. And Aristotle clearly directs us to emulate, in our own lives and circumstances ("relative to us") the wisdom of such individuals.

John Rawls, in his hugely influential *A Theory of Justice*, puts such emulation into Aristotelian psychological context in what he calls the Aristotelian Principle: "other things being equal, human beings enjoy the exercise of their realized capacities (their innate or trained abilities), and this enjoyment increases the more the capacity is realized, or the greater its complexity."[11] This has a developmental dimension which Rawls describes as a psychological law: "as a person's capacities increase over time (brought about by physiological and biological maturation, for example, the development of the nervous system in a young child), and as he trains these capacities and learns how to exercise them, he will in due course come to prefer the more complex activities that he can now engage in which call upon his newly realized abilities."[12] But most importantly to our purposes, this Aristotelian Principle has a companion effect: "as we witness the exercise of well-trained abilities by others, these displays are enjoyed by us and arouse a desire that we should do the same things ourselves. *We want to be like those persons who can exercise the abilities that we find latent in our nature.*"[13]

Happily, in his *Rhetoric*, Aristotle offers a brief but dense discussion of emulation (*zēlos*, from which is derived the English *zeal*, or fervor in pursuit of something). First, he defines emulation as an emotion of "pain caused by seeing the presence, in persons whose nature is like our own, of good things that are highly valued and are possible for ourselves to acquire; but it is felt not because others have these goods, but because we have not got them ourselves" [1388b]. Aristotle then elaborates on this last qualification by describing emulation as "a good feeling felt by good persons," to be distinguished from envy, "a bad feeling felt by bad persons." Furthermore, "emulation makes us take steps to secure the good things in question, [while] envy makes us take steps to stop our neighbor having them" [1388b]. In emulation, we see the good things that others possess but we do not, and are moved to acquire them for ourselves (but not by dispossessing our neighbor). As Rawls remarks, "the Aristotelian Principle is a principle of motivation."[14]

But what are these "good things," the objects of emulation? Aristotle answers: "excellence in its various forms . . . and also all those good things that are useful and serviceable to others. . . . those good things our possession of which can give enjoyment to our neighbors" [1388b]. And what persons are the objects of the feeling? Those of course who possess the good things already mentioned, but also "courage, wisdom, public office." More simply (and again, in a circular fashion), the emulable are "those whom many people wish to be like; . . . those whom many admire, or whom we ourselves admire; and those who have been praised and eulogized by poets or prose-writers" [1388b]. We look to the best among us to understand what it means to be fully human according to our own tradition—and we emulate them. We want for ourselves those qualities we admire in exemplary others.

Updating Aristotle's "Good Things"

A contemporary version of Aristotle's emulable "good things" is provided by Anne Colby's and William Damon's criteria for the identification of moral exemplars in their now-classic study, *Some Do Care: Contemporary Lives of Moral Commitment*. It is not too much of a stretch to describe Colby's and Damon's hope for their study as contributing to our understanding of the dynamics of emulation. They "recognized the outstanding societal contributions of great moral leaders such as Mahatma Gandhi, Andrei Sakharov, and Mother Teresa." Understanding how such "epitomes of human moral excellence . . . acquire such excellence could open a pathway toward moral progress, both for individuals and society."[15] To achieve this understanding, they first had to develop criteria for identifying moral leaders, persons who would be available for research interviews. Their extensive consultations with 22 doctrinally diverse experts in ethical reflection—theologians, philosophers, and other scholars—resulted in the following criteria, "good things," which genuine moral exemplars would necessarily possess:

1. A sustained commitment to moral ideals or principles that include a generalized respect for humanity; or a sustained evidence of moral virtue
2. A disposition to act in accord with one's moral ideals or principles, implying also a consistency between one's actions and intentions and between the means and ends of one's actions
3. A willingness to risk one's self-interest for the sake of one's moral values
4. A tendency to be inspiring to others and thereby to move them to moral action

5. A sense of realistic humility about one's own importance relative to the world at large, implying a relative lack of concern for one's own ego.[16]

Of these five criteria—which I have abbreviated, respectively, commitment to humanity, integrity, courage, charisma, and humility—the fourth, charisma, is especially and obviously relevant to the Aristotelian theme of emulation and therefore to moral education centered on exemplars. Although I have not systematically measured against these criteria the figures selected for study in the course, I believe this could be done successfully in almost all cases.

But perhaps more important for this chapter than identifying moral exemplars in any definitive way, whether ancient or modern,[17] is the question of who are the most likely *subjects* of emulation. Such a distressing but praiseworthy emotion, according to Aristotle, tends to be felt "by persons who believe themselves to *deserve* certain good things that they have not got. . . . It is accordingly felt by the *young* and by persons of *lofty* dispositions" [1388b; emphasis added]. In the following section of the *Rhetoric*, Aristotle gives us a portrait of "the youthful type of character" that seems partially to conflate the young (the post-pubescent, because he refers to their sexual desires) and those of lofty dispositions. Although it is hardly a wholly complimentary portrait (e.g., "they are changeable and fickle in their desires"), the young, it is said, "have exalted notions, because they have not yet been humbled by life or learnt its necessary limitations; moreover their hopeful disposition makes them think themselves equal to great things. . . . They would always rather do noble deeds than useful ones: their lives are regulated more by their character than by reasoning; and whereas reasoning leads us to choose what is useful, excellence [or virtue] leads us to choose what is noble" [1389a].

The young, at least those who may be said to be on the path to excellence of character, because of their lofty (if fickle) dispositions, are especially prone to emulation, to the influence of admirable (and charismatic) persons. Perhaps aware of an incipient or potential excellence, they believe themselves deserving of those goods they see in exemplary persons. (I'll return to this theme of desert later.) Such young people, Aristotle implies, are thus strikingly open to change and motivated toward personal growth. A similar observation about young people today comes from a very different source.

Liminality in Three Dimensions: The College Years, Young Adults, and Saints as Exemplars

Contemporary U.S. student culture has been described as demonstrating "liminality" and the college experience itself as a "rite of passage." According to cultural anthropologist Rebekah Nathan,[18] "rites of passage have universal characteristics marked by severance from one's normal status, entrance into a 'liminal' state where normal rules of society are lifted, and finally reintegration into society within a new status. . . . It is in the middle or 'liminal' state—the ambiguous state of being neither here nor there—that anthropologists see profoundly creative and transformative possibilities."[19] These anthropological concepts can be applied to the U.S. college, in which "undergraduate culture itself becomes this liminal communal space where students bond with one another, sometimes for life, and, amid rules of suspended normality and often hardship, explore their identities, wrestle with their parents' world, and wonder about their future."[20] The experiences of such liminality will be of great relevance to any pedagogy with personal development and social transformation as a goal, for they "may help to liberate 'the human capacities of cognition, affect, volition, creativity' and thereby prompt innovative responses to the social system, and to the feelings of alienation, exploitation, and divisiveness that it may spawn."[21]

In remarkably similar language, Kristján Kristjánsson observes that "Aristotle's 'emulation' has affective, conative [volitional], cognitive and behavioural [creative?] elements built into it."[22] He elaborates on these elements as follows:

> In the context of role-model [or moral-exemplar] education, the *affective* element would be a kind of pain at my relative lack of a desired quality, possessed by the role model; the *conative* element would be the motivation

> to acquire such a quality (without, of course, taking anything away from the role model); the *cognitive* element would consist of the development of an understanding of why this quality, displayed to a pronounced degree by the role model, is something that I deem morally worthy of being valued by me, and what reasonable ways there are for me to transform myself in order to acquire it; and the *behavioural* element would involve the actual striving for this quality.[23]

The deliberate provocation of emulation in the loftily disposed young through the study of moral exemplars in a traditional college setting with its liminality and potential for the liberation or development of the human capacities of cognition, affect, volition, and creativity—of the whole person, to use Ignatian language—would therefore seem to represent a powerful pedagogy. But we can add at least one more dynamic to that mix, and that comes from the analogy between moral exemplars and saints.

Although saints are not simply exemplars and not all saints are imitable in their sometimes miraculous displays of holiness,[24] exemplariness has been described by scholars of religion as one of sainthood's essential features. John Stratton Hawley, for example, drawing upon the teaching of the Roman Catholic Church's Second Vatican Council, lays out the three functions of the saint (cross-culturally) as example, fellowship, and aid. A saint is "a model, a prototype, not merely an example, but an exemplar . . . a paradigm that sets the shape for a series of imitative phenomena that follow in its wake." But the exemplariness of the saint can be understood in "two divergent senses." In one sense, "the saintly example instantiates and thus clarifies general principles of morality and qualities of character that can be articulated as meaningful and understood as possible for all participants in a society or community of faith."[25]

But "in its second sense, by contrast, the saintly exemplar does not always accord so easily with the moral standards which articulate a culture's highest sense of itself. Often saints do not just heighten ordinary morality. They implicitly question it by seeming to embody a strange, higher standard that does not quite fit with the moral system that governs ordinary propriety and often cannot be articulated in normal discourse."[26] The example provided is St. Francis, not in his inimitably miraculous stigmata, but in his stripping himself naked "before the good people of Assisi" and especially before his materialistic father, a textile merchant, in order to demonstrate loyalty to a different Father and a higher standard of values. Nothing humanly inimitable in that, but it seems unlikely that any of those good townspeople went and did likewise.

As John Coleman puts it, "saints, as liminal figures, function to break down and transform ordinary notions of virtue."[27] Saints are "'the very ones who seem so unlike us, . . . the ones in whom the virtues are normatively displayed, the people against whom our own goodness must be measured.'"[28] This same theme is emphasized by Lawrence Cunningham, in whose understanding the saint "serves both a paradigmatic and prophetic function."[29] Novelist Ron Hansen applies this idea to the founder of the Jesuits: "We are challenged by Ignatius in much the same way that he was challenged by Francis and Dominic. And that may be the best purpose for books of saints: to have our complacency and mediocrity goaded, and to highlight our lame urge to go forward with the familiar rather than the difficult and serious. We often find tension and unease with the holy lives we read about because there is always an implicit criticism of our habits and weaknesses in greatness and achievement."[30]

Flescher observes that when he has taught Dorothy Day (cofounder of the Catholic Worker movement), his "students who admire Day's deeds often find themselves confronted by her words. They want to hold her in esteem for the works of mercy that she regularly performs, but they do not see, as she sees so vividly, how the kind of self-transformation that would enable them to become likewise is for them realistic or even possible. The more seriously students take her words, the more they feel indicted for not exploring the possible, and the more tension that already exists between word and deed increases."[31] Thus, Dorothy Day, one particular moral exemplar, has been both a paradigmatic and a prophetic figure for Flescher's students—and, I would add, for me and mine.

To the extent that we can translate from the moral exemplariness of the saint to the nonsaintly or even nonreligious moral exemplar, we can suggest that the latter serves a similar dual function as paradigm and prophet. On the one hand, the exemplar embodies norms or virtues that may transcend conventional morality (so important a goal of justice education)—and on the other, the exemplar critiques the individual's achievement of the same.

Aristotelian Desert or Aristotelian Shame?

No wonder that Aristotle describes emulation as painful or distressing. Aristotle, however, understood that feeling in the context of personal desert: "I am a good person who deserves the good things that I see other good persons possess"—and not of personal shortcoming—"I am not the compassionate, committed person of conviction I could be, as I can see by way of contrast with the achievements of Albert Schweitzer or Dorothy Day." Indeed, this latter understanding of emulation is closer to Aristotle's own concept of shame, the feeling of the young person who is brought to a painful recognition of his or her own moral underdevelopment. In the *Nicomachean Ethics*, Aristotle describes shame, "a kind of fear of dishonour," as "more like a passion than a state of character," because "people who feel disgraced blush," a bodily condition, "which is thought to be characteristic of passion rather than a state of character" [1128b]. The Ross translation of the *Nicomachean Ethics* calls shame a "quasi-virtue" [the heading given to IV.9], and Burnyeat describes the feeling as "the semivirtue of the learner."[32] Aristotle observes that "the passion is not becoming to every age, but only to youth," and "we praise young people who are prone to [it] . . . for young people commit many errors but are restrained by shame." Shame therefore "may be said to be conditionally a good thing" [1128b] because it serves as a corrective at the all-important level of *pathé* (affect or emotion) in the process of becoming virtuous.

The burden of Aristotle's argument seems to be that shame *motivates* a learner to try harder. It is superior to fear of punishment as a motivation since shameful "actions pain him *internally*, not consequentially. He is therefore receptive to the kind of moral education which will set his judgment straight and develop his intellectual capacities (practical wisdom) which will enable him to avoid such errors" in the future.[33] Shame in the young is a sign that moral development is taking place; but in the mature, a sign that moral development has faltered because the virtuous person will not commit bad actions, and will therefore have no cause to feel ashamed. The shame of the young person, however, is the appropriate affective response to having done unjust, ignoble—shameful—acts. It presents him or her with a choice of whether or not to recommit to "learning to be good."[34]

This implicit convergence of emulation and shame in Aristotle has been noted by Kristjánsson:

> [S]trictly speaking, emulation is not, any more than shame, according to Aristotle's description, a virtue of the fully virtuous—for they will have nothing morally worthy left to strive for, nor anything to be ashamed of—but rather of those on the way to virtue. Much like shame, emulation is thus a virtue characteristic of the young. However, that makes emulation obviously more, rather than less, salient from the perspective of moral education.[35]

In my many years of teaching moral exemplars, I have never heard a student suggest that she "deserves" more courage because she is a good person like Rev. Martin Luther King, Jr., who had more of this good thing than she. On the other hand, I have heard many students say, in effect, that they just don't know whether they could ever be even fleetingly as courageous as Dr. King obviously was consistently. As one student confessed in a reflection written for a section in which Oscar Romero, the martyred archbishop of El Salvador, was the moral exemplar under study, "When looking at what Romero had done with his life and how he essentially gave his life to others, I feel very self-centered about what I have done in my life thus far."[36] There is something like shame in that self-recognition. Students are imagining themselves trying and perhaps failing to be more than they presently are, "thus far." Such shame is the first step of emulation.[37]

Although Mev Puleo was several years out of college at the time, she, too, experienced shame ("disgrace") when she compared herself with her own personal litany of prophetic exemplars, from peasant pastoral activists to bishops and theologians, in the progressive Brazilian Catholic Church. But she also begs strength from them:

> The communion of saints. Toinho, Goreth, Sylvia, Dom Pedro [Bishop Casaldáliga], Clodovis [Boff], Carlos Mesters—all. You are a mirror, and it sometimes chills me and embarrasses me to look at myself in your light. I feel disgrace, a need for mercy, a need for your strength to pull forth to me. You who have lived through death threats and dictatorships, monstrous bishops and abuse from Mother Church, you who walk daily attending Lazarus's wounds. Help me. Move me. Be with me. We are one. Yes, the struggle is one. The struggle is one.[38]

Why is this imaginative encounter of the young person with the exemplar so important? To quote Kristjánsson again, the good things possessed by the exemplar,

> those morally worthy qualities would, in principle, be recognizable and morally justifiable independent of the role model. Yet, there is, in fact, in the Aristotelian model no other way for young people of getting to know those qualities and learning to emulate them than by following the example of the role model. Its exemplariness is thus a contingent fact that helps the role model fulfill the all-important role of representing and conveying moral virtue.[39]

In the words of Dan Hartnett, S.J.: "Few of us would probably ever commit to justice or risk a new course of action were it not for certain witnesses to justice who have preceded us. People like Mahatma Gandhi, Thich Nhat Hanh, Dorothy Day, Abraham Heschel, Mother Teresa, and Oscar Romero. . . ."[40] To put it simply: No exemplars, no emulation; no emulation, no *new* moral exemplars.

Summary

To this point, I have briefly presented MacIntyre on the self in community and tradition as a general context for the teaching of moral exemplars. I then explored in some depth the Aristotelian theme of emulation in the young as one way of understanding what might be happening when a college student encounters a moral exemplar in a course of study. I have denied any Charlie Brown-like theory of simple, mechanical imitation. I have suggested that the concept of liminality—of the young person in his or her own developmental readiness, of the traditional college context as a time and place set apart, and of the transcendent status of the exemplar *vis-à-vis* conventional morality—provides a rich matrix in which to understand the potential power of a course such as "Faith and Moral Development." And I have amended Aristotle's description of emulation by emphasizing not personal desert but something like the Aristotelian semi-virtue of shame. Two of these themes, of measuring oneself against one's potential or against one's own highest ideal, and of moving beyond conventional or ordinary morality, deserve further exploration. My primary sources for this reflection will be, respectively, Nietzche's comments on moral exemplars in *Schopenhauer as Educator* and Andrew Michael Flescher's philosophical monograph, *Heroes, Saints, and Ordinary Morality*.

Nietzsche on Moral Exemplars and the Higher Self

In his essay "Nietzsche's Perfectionism," James Conant excerpts "the focal passage" on moral exemplars from *Schopenhauer as Educator*:

> If the genius in art is always the first, the throng of imitators being always in his train, in morality, each agent has the prerogative of genius. . . . [H]e who "imitates" the example of a moral creator or a sublime model is in his turn a creator. . . . The imitator of the [artistic] genius is a simple talent; but the imitator of a hero is himself a hero.[41]

Arguing that this passage has often been misunderstood (as elitist), Conant asks three questions that will help elucidate Nietzsche's concept of an exemplar: "(1) Who are *my* exemplars? (2) What is (or should be) my *relation* to an exemplar? (3) *What* does an exemplar disclose?" (p. 202; emphasis in original).

Taking the questions in reverse order, Conant quotes Nietzsche in answer to the third question:

> "It is hard to create in anyone this condition of intrepid self-knowledge because it is impossible to teach love; for it is love alone that can bestow on the soul, not only a clear, discriminating and self-contemptuous view of itself, but also the desire to look beyond itself and to seek with all its might for a higher self as yet still concealed from it." (p. 202)

As Conant parses this passage, "your 'higher self,' according to [Nietzsche], comes into view only through your confrontation with what you trust and admire in an exemplary other" (pp. 202–03). Despite Nietzsche's harsher language of self-contempt, the resonances in this passage with Aristotelian emulation, shame, and *telos* are rich. Love for what is higher in the exemplary other reveals to us our own "higher self," the exemplary person or moral hero we could become. But with Nietzsche as for Aristotle, it is a difficult discovery. We likely do not want to know that we are not (yet) who we should be.

That begins to answer the second question: What is (or should be) my *relation* to an exemplar? Here Conant refers to "a critical concept for Nietzsche: . . . a distinctively self-revelatory sort of shame." What seems to set Nietzsche apart from Aristotle is that for him, "the characteristic mark of this sort of shame is that one is able to experience it—that is, feel genuinely ashamed of who or what one is—without thereby experiencing the feeling of distress that ordinarily accompanies shame. The role of the exemplar is to occasion the experience of this distinctive sort of shame" (p. 204). Conant contrasts Nietzsche not with Aristotle but with a very Aristotelian-sounding Kant, for whom "moral shame is an emotion that one strives to overcome (or avoid) through the cultivation of virtue; whereas Nietzschean impersonal shame is an emotion that one strives to engender in oneself so as to overcome (or avoid) a false sense of virtue" (p. 205). This is a fine distinction, indeed, and perhaps not one that requires an either/or choice. Presumably countering false virtue and cultivating genuine virtue go hand in hand, and both can be engendered by encountering a moral exemplar.

Similarly, it may be a fine distinction to claim that moral shame occurs without distress. The point seems to be that Nietzsche celebrates the discovery of a higher self occasioned by encounter with a moral exemplar in a way that Aristotle could honor only in the young. Again, I don't see the necessity of an either/or choice. Even in adults, may not the shame engendered by encounter with a moral exemplar include both a painful revelation of who we now are and an inspiring revelation of who we might become? Conant himself acknowledges the dual and even contradictory nature of self-revelation, its horror and its exhilaration, when he writes that "the horror is tied to the thought of the past (what we have thus far made of our lives). The exhilaration is tied to the thought of the future (what we have now learned we can make of our lives)" (p. 208). Surely, the pain of such revelations is one of the reasons why self-knowledge is so hard to embrace—especially because elsewhere in *Schopenhauer as Educator*, Nietzsche writes that "it is a painful and dangerous undertaking to dig down into oneself in this way and to descend violently and directly into the shaft of one's being."[42] It is difficult to know exactly what Nietzsche means by an "impersonal" shame except that he seems to emphasize the affirmative and future-oriented over the negative and past-oriented: as if that did away with the pain, as if self-contempt were not distressing.

That brings us to Conant's third question: Who are your exemplars? He answers immediately: "They are those individuals who are able to trigger this experience of impersonal shame in you" (p. 206). The emphasis here is on *you*, or to use the language of Aristotle's definition of virtue: Our moral exemplars are those who *are so relative to us*, at our particular stage of development, given our particular individuality, and not simply in some generic or universal way. "To treat an exemplar as a model for mere imitation is to fail faithfully to follow oneself. . . . Nietzsche's later paradoxical notion that you should faithfully follow your own footsteps finds its equivalent [in *Schopenhauer as Educator*] in the notion that there is a path along which no one can go but you, . . . that there is no answer to the question 'Whither does it lead?' until you have gone along it" (p. 206).

"Hero-worship," that is, "is interpreted by Nietzsche as a strategy for evading an inwardly felt demand for self-transformation through the cultivating of ethically impotent forms of admiration" (p. 209). A mimetic relationship to exemplars is not only psychologically naïve (*à la* Charlie Brown) but also ethically regressive, leading perhaps to that false sense of virtue which our encounters with moral exemplars ought to undermine. As Flescher observes, "to claim an appreciation for [an exemplar like Dorothy] Day and then fail to look inward is to engage in a moral evasion."[43] One of my own students expresses this difficult insight well; she is speaking of Dr. Paul Farmer, whose life and medical work among the poorest of the poor, especially in Haiti, is the subject of Tracy Kidder's *Mountains Beyond Mountains*:

> "Paul is a model of what should be done. He's not a model for how it has to be done."[44] I appreciate Jim Kim's comments concerning the fact that many including myself look to Farmer as a model. At the same time, however, we often allow ourselves to stand in awe of his accomplishments which seem beyond our own capabilities. We may place Farmer on a pedestal without even trying to implement change for the better. Oftentimes, I am guilty of this method which seems to be the lazy way of reacting to figures like Farmer. I find it much easier to simply admire from afar. When I realize that Farmer's example serves to challenge me to act I become uncomfortable. As a part of my human nature I do not want to feel discomfort. However, sometimes I need to feel uneasy in order to act for change.[45]

Of course, encounter with moral exemplarity and revelation of a higher self is not a one-time thing. It is, rather, a life-time thing, at least for those of us who do not enter adulthood as fully virtuous. In this perspective, young adulthood and the college years are an opportunity (of liminality in its several dimensions) to take ownership of this long-term process and project. As Conant puts it, Nietzsche "pictures each of us as a series of such [split] selves, each in flight from, and yet each also representing a stepping stone toward, its own unique, exemplary successor," (p. 203) one's own higher self. That developmental, life-span perspective takes us from Nietzsche back to the Aristotelian worldview, this time as elaborated by Andrew Michael Flescher.

Heroes, Saints, and Ordinary Morality: The Developmental Imperative

The purpose of Flescher's impressive book is to answer the question, "'Why read about heroes and saints?'" His hypothesis is "that we ought to read about heroes and saints because they, who were once not so heroic or saintly, have struggled just as we have but have subsequently learned to lead a virtuous life. . . . We ought to read about heroes and saints because of their potential to serve as mentors for those interested in living a virtuous life."[46] Much of his book is concerned with the philosophical literature and debate on supererogation over the past half-century. In a nutshell: Are ordinary people called to go beyond the call of duty, of a minimal moral obligation, as do extraordinary people like heroes and saints? But for our purposes, his most important contribution is his elaboration of "the thesis of moral development." Flescher's own answer to that question, over against the supererogationist No and the anti-supererogationist Yes, is a *qualified* supererogationist Yes *and* No. Between the Yes and the No is the thesis of moral development. In its simplest form, the thesis can be stated as follows: "The point of speculating about ideally virtuous persons [and of teaching moral exemplars], . . . is not to get us to emulate them immediately [which would be psychologically unrealistic], but rather to motivate us to become more critical with respect to our own moral progress."[47]

Stated more formally, the thesis presented in *Heroes, Saints, and Ordinary Morality* is "that our sense of duty ought to expand over time, that we should strive to dispose ourselves to go above and beyond duty when possible, and that the scope of what we consider to be supererogatory correspondingly ought to diminish as we acquire an expanded sense of duty and cultivate the disposition to go above and beyond."[48] One day's supererogation becomes another day's duty. In effect, Rawls's *descriptive* Aristotelian Principle becomes *prescriptive*. Because we *can* grow in virtue, we *ought* to grow in virtue. Because we can admire an Albert Schweitzer or a Dorothy Day, even if we can't (and even shouldn't try to) copy them immediately, we ought to emulate them—or rather, their virtues—ever more closely over a lifetime of striving for personal moral betterment. In its most condensed form, the thesis of moral development states that we have a "meta-duty" always to become more virtuous. As Flescher remarks, "deontic [duty] and aretaic [virtue] concepts are thus importantly related to one another."[49] According to the thesis of moral development, duty and virtue are dynamically related, not conceptually opposed, as is sometimes assumed. A cartoon in *The New Yorker* (see Figure 6.1) captures this imperative nicely.

What, from the point of view of the thesis of moral development, is the purpose of studying the lives of moral exemplars? It is, to restate

"I want to be a better person, but then what — a much better person?"

Figure 6.1
(© Erik Hilgerdt/The New Yorker Collection/www.cartoonbank.com)

an earlier point, "that we ought to read about heroes and saints because they, who were once not so heroic or saintly, have struggled just as we have but have subsequently learned to lead a virtuous life. . . . We ought to read about heroes and saints because of their potential to serve as mentors for those interested in living a virtuous life."[50] In studying narratives of exemplary persons, we observe not just their virtues but especially their struggles to *be* virtuous. It may be distressing or shameful to have to acknowledge our lack of virtue compared to the exemplars, but because their own "painful pathway[s] to virtue"[51] are so evident in their narratives, we cannot dismiss them as ontologically extraordinary and therefore irrelevant to our ordinary lives. They were not born with a virtue-gene that we lack. Indeed, "we come to see moral development as an ever-present task" in the narratives of the exemplary and therefore also necessarily in our own lives. And that task "entails our coming to cultivate a kind of 'moral angst' about our present level of accomplishment."[52] At the very least, we can—and therefore must—emulate their exemplary strivings. As the recently beatified martyr Franz Jägerstätter wrote, "For us men there are only two possibilities in this world: either we become ever better or ever worse; there is simply no such thing as standing still."[53]

Conclusion

Flescher sums it up nicely: "Regardless of whether the moral virtuosi we encounter become our mentors, at the very least their existence stands as a challenge to the ways in which we become accustomed to conceiving our responsibility in society. Such exemplars are not simply anomalies. When we encounter them, we are forced to ask ourselves how we are living our lives, as well as whether we ought to exercise a choice or series of choices that for them is no longer an option."[54] Philip Hallie reports that Magda Trocmé, a leader in the rescue of some 5,000 Jews from the Nazis during World War II, "does not believe that there is such a thing as moral nobility that sets off some people—the saints—from others—the common, decent people.

. . . [S]he does not believe in works of supererogation, deeds of extraordinarily high value. . . . There are only people who accept responsibility, and those who do not. For her, as for them, a person either opens the door or closes it in the face of a victim."[55] Or, as Dorothy Day famously said, "Don't call me a saint. I don't want to be dismissed that easily."

"Faith and Moral Development," for these many years, has been my attempt to create a pedagogical context, within a university setting, in which students have the opportunity to study moral exemplars and not to dismiss them too easily, as totally unlike themselves, but as ordinary persons becoming extraordinary. It has been my attempt to launch these young adults on the sometimes painful, often joyous, and always challenging pathway to virtue. I have been teaching moral exemplars in not just one but two senses. As one of my students in this course wrote in a weekly reflection:

> The FMD classes are working. . . . They make me think, and thinking is dangerous. They give me examples and examples are empowering. They plant seeds that are self fertilized and breaking at the seams to move to the next stage. They have ruined me from mainstream society just like this Jesuit school and my trip to third world countries have "ruined" me. But I'm glad I've been ruined. Now my life can begin.[56]

A Personal Postscript: In Class with Romero

Since 1995, I have taught some 50 sections of "Faith and Moral Development," an upper-division undergraduate seminar at Creighton University and also a required course in the Justice and Peace Studies Program that I direct.[57] The course is innovative in several respects, but particularly in subject matter because we study personal exemplars of faith and moral development and various theoretical perspectives on that development.

Recently, the case study for one section was Archbishop Oscar Romero of El Salvador. We read two books: *Romero: A Life*, by James

Brockman, S.J. (2005), and *A Sacred Voice Is Calling: Personal Vocation and Social Conscience*, by John Neafsey (2006). Despite the centrality of Romero to my own sense of vocation, this was the first time that I had taught a course on the archbishop. Indeed, the previous summer was the first time I had read Romero's biography although I certainly knew the outline of his story from the powerful film "Romero," starring Raul Julia. That was enough to help change my life. I became a Catholic, discovered a vocation in social justice ministry and education, and moved my young family across the country so that I could study at Weston Jesuit School of Theology, then in Cambridge, Massachusetts.

A Model and Guide

I think I was afraid that getting closer to Romero by reading his biography would be too demanding, would set the bar (or should I say, *the cross*?) way too high. But after visiting our son, who was then a student in the Santa Clara University *Casa de la Solidaridad* program in San Salvador in March 2006, and after visiting Romero's small apartment and the chapel of the cancer hospital for the poor where he fell to an assassin's bullet on March 24, 1980, I could no longer keep him at a safe distance. I screwed "my courage to the sticking place" (as Lady Macbeth put it) and ordered the Brockman book.

Midway through that semester, during one of our first sessions together, a wonderfully simpatico spiritual director asked me where or how I had experienced consolation and desolation over the last month. As he allowed me quietly to settle into that question, I felt welling up within me the very Ignatian experience of tears. Gradually regaining my composure, I suggested that teaching the life of Oscar Romero, the one figure above all others who had brought me into the life of Christ as an adult, had given me—and was giving me at that very moment—an experience of both consolation and desolation.

I was consoled, as I had been when I first heard Romero's story, because he made it plain that it is possible to live a life of profound Christian integrity and commitment to the kingdom in our day. But 27 years of my own vocation and one biography later, I knew much more intimately, if still at some distance, what that integrity had cost Romero, even before his death. As Ignacio Ellacuría, S.J. has said, in the person of Archbishop Romero, God visited El Salvador. That visit, that life, conformed to the life and passion of El Salvador (the Savior) almost 2,000 years before. That was deeply consoling. Christ had risen again magnificently in a humble priest from the hinterlands of a poor developing country.

Desolation and the Dark Spirit

Yet my experience of Oscar Romero 24 years after I had become a Catholic was also one of desolation. I was too timid to take Oscar as my confirmation name. One of my students expressed my own feelings well: "When looking at what Romero had done with his life and how he essentially gave his life to others, I feel very self-centered about what I have done in my life thus far." In the midst of a vicious civil war, often in bitter dispute with a majority of his fellow Salvadoran bishops and with the papal nuncio, libeled repeatedly and outrageously in the reactionary national press and seen as suspect by some in the Vatican, and with his life under constant threat, Romero grew stronger, deeper, and more prophetic. Accused of betraying the Gospel of love and justice for self-promotion, ideology, or even terrorism, Romero lived it out ever more authentically. By comparison, in my comfortable circumstances, I seemed a fraud.

Desolation is the work of what Ignatius called the "dark spirit" of the Enemy, of the anti-kingdom. I have been learning the hard way just how seductive, perverse, and persistent the voice that insinuates "Fraud!" can be. I know the need to confront that dark voice head-on. But I also know that Ignatius instructs the retreatant in the first week of the Spiritual Exercises to pray for the grace of shame and confusion—the only sane, honest responses to one's own complicity in the sin against God's world. What was I experiencing in my relationship to Oscar Romero: consolation from God, desolation from the Enemy, or the grace of honest self-assessment? So I made my own prayer:

> God, grant me the grace to accept, with gratitude,
> shame and confusion when they come from you,

courage to resist them when they come from the Enemy,
and the wisdom to discern the one from the other.

I do not pretend to know fully what goes on in the hearts and consciences—the "secret core and sanctuary," in the words of Vatican II[58]—of my students in this course. Occasionally, they give me glimpses of something like consolation, which they feel when inspired by exemplars and saints like Oscar Romero or Dorothy Day. Because the world they are about to enter as idealistic young adults is riddled with injustice, violence, and suffering, such guides and models are crucial. And occasionally they allow me to glimpse something of the shame and confusion they feel in the very same context. God help us, we are not yet who we need to be.

I once heard that teachers should never give students an assignment that they themselves have not undertaken. To that, I say Amen.

PART III INSTITUTION AND PROGRAM

7 Education for Justice and the Catholic University

Innovation or Development? An Argument from Tradition

> The challenge of Christian humanism remains central to the task of achieving the identity of Catholic universities. But today that humanism must be a social humanism, a humanism that recognizes that it must address not only [the] heights to which human culture can rise but also the depths of suffering into which societies can descend.
>
> *David Hollenbach, S.J.*[1]

The previous chapter concludes Part II, in which the foundational insights and themes developed in the three chapters of Part I—on personal encounter, the Pedagogical Circle, and Catholic justice pedagogy as a MacIntyrian social practice—were seen to be variously at work in three justice pedagogies in university settings: cross-cultural immersion, service-learning, and the study of moral exemplars. In Part III, I turn to issues of Institution and Program. Chapter 7 addresses the foundational question of the place of justice education within the Catholic university. Does it belong at the heart of the university or in campus ministry only? Chapter 8 is summative but also explores the theme of shame more deeply, offers one model of what the Pedagogical Circle might look like within a university curriculum, gives students within that program a chance to speak, and concludes with some reflections on young adult vocational development.

The Commitment to Justice as Constitutive of the Catholic University

The preceding chapters assume that justice education is proper to a Catholic university and that Catholic social teaching should provide not just the subject matter of an elective course in the theology department or the animating spirit in some campus ministry activities but also a perspective that pervades the culture and ethos of the entire university, in its teaching, its research, and its "way of proceeding," in the classic Jesuit phrase.[2] The argument from magisterial doctrine for education for justice in the Catholic university is clear: *if* "action on behalf of justice and participation in the transformation of the world . . . [is] . . . a constitutive dimension of the preaching of the Gospel, or, in other words, of the Church's mission for the redemption of the human race and its liberation from every oppressive situation,"[3] *and if* the Catholic university finds its own particular mission within that broader mission,[4] *then it follows* that such a university must also constitute itself according to the demands of justice, as understood by the Catholic tradition. Of course, it must do so "*universitariamente*"[5]—in the manner of a university and not as a social service agency or political party.

The Catholic university had a long history of educating for justice before the late nineteenth-century advent of modern Catholic social teaching (CST). What, then, are the warrants or precedents, if any, for the contemporary focus on justice in Catholic higher education? Is this an innovation or a development? In answering these questions, this chapter will focus on justice education proper and also on the formation and learning of its students, but not on justice and research or on justice and the university's way of proceeding as an institution.[6] My basic thesis is that the educational models developed by Saint Ignatius of Loyola, founder of the Society of Jesus, and John Henry Cardinal Newman, author of the classic *The Idea of a University*, two major sources from the deep tradition of Catholic higher education, demonstrate that concern for what we now call "social justice" has long been a fundamental dimension of the Catholic university in its relationship to its students, and who those students are and are becoming, as a matter of intellectual and moral formation.

Although this argument has gained ground in recent years[7] to the point that references to educating for justice appear in institutional marketing, it is my impression that even as spoken resistance is waning, many members of the Catholic university community still privately believe that justice education is an innovation and even a departure from, if not a betrayal of, the traditional mission of higher education, Catholic or otherwise. They think that the mission should be focused on truth—whether understood as the transmission of the honored truths of the past (as preserved in the so-called "Western canon") or as the pursuit of new truths (as modeled in the most prestigious research institutions) and not on justice. But this is surely not an either/or proposition. I will respond to this critique, however muted it may have become, from the tradition of Catholic higher education itself. Even those sympathetic to this commitment may not be aware of its pedigree. A concluding section will explore briefly how this tradition has been reinvigorated and implemented in the contemporary Catholic university.

Probably no source is cited more often in discussions of the mission of the university than Cardinal Newman's *The Idea of a University*.[8] I will argue that this influential work of the nineteenth century, despite being associated mainly with the idea of knowledge for its own sake and not for its practical or social value, actually presents an impassioned plea for *both* truth and justice as guiding values of the Catholic university. An even earlier tradition is Saint Ignatius of Loyola's groundbreaking practice of higher education developed during the period of Renaissance humanism. I will demonstrate that here, too, the transmission and pursuit of truth will be seen to converge with commitment to moral formation and social uplift.

These historical explorations will make apparent the twofold nature of education for justice: education *of* the poor and marginalized for their social advancement, and education of the nonpoor and privileged young not only for their entry into the professions but also *on behalf of* the poor and marginalized—on behalf of justice. In both cases, such educational commitments enrich the common good as a matter of the Catholic university's essential mission.

John Henry Newman's *The Idea of a University*: Teaching Universal Knowledge

John Henry Newman died in 1890, one year before the founding of the modern Catholic social teaching tradition with the publication of *Rerum Novarum*[9] (also known as *On the Condition of Labor*), the great social encyclical of Pope Leo XIII. (Leo had named Newman a cardinal in 1879.) Given his supremely high valuation of the authority of the papacy (p. 10), Newman would have taken *Rerum Novarum* and its successor documents with great seriousness. But I will argue that Newman's idea of a university has room in it for CST intrinsically, and not just extrinsically, not just as a matter of obedience to the Magisterium. Newman was aware of the social mission of the Catholic university.

In his preface, Newman makes his view of a university as plain and direct as possible: "it is a place of *teaching* universal *knowledge*. This implies that its object is, on the one hand, intellectual not moral; and, on the other, that it is the diffusion and extension of knowledge rather than the advancement." To drive home these points, he observes that if the university's "object were scientific and philosophical discovery, I do not see why a University should have students; if religious training, I do not see how it can be the seat of literature and science" (p. xxxvii; emphasis in original).

The logic of these exclusive categories may not be persuasive to academics today, when it is assumed that great universities are so because they are great *research* institutions and when even small universities and colleges with heavy teaching loads also expect their faculty to publish. Newman, however, denies the teacher/scholar model that more or less explicitly underlies such modern institutional demands (p. xl). In fact, during his seven-year tenure as the founding rector (president) of the new Catholic University of Ireland, Newman "strove . . . to provide for research as well as good teaching."[10] Newman's practice, if not his theory, saves his "idea" from dismissal by contemporary academics as too narrow for contemporary application.

However, Newman's argument that the object of a university is intellectual, not moral, and that moral education is equivalent to religious training, is likely to meet with less resistance from some university people. Clearly that is the issue in *The Idea of a University* with which I must contend, justice education being a species of moral education. It is crucial that we understand what Newman meant by what is now the stock phrase, "knowledge for its own sake," or, as he titles Discourse V, "Knowledge Its Own End," the very object of a university or liberal education.

Knowledge for the Sake of . . .?

Newman gives us hints of the full meaning or purpose of a university education in his preface when he turns to the theme of the Holy See's wish to see a Catholic university begun in Ireland. The Pope's "first and chief and direct object is, not science, art, professional skill, literature, the discovery of knowledge, but some benefit or other, to accrue, by means of literature and science, *to his own children*; . . . their exercise and growth in certain habits, *moral* or intellectual" (pp. xxxviii–xxxix; emphasis added). Perhaps surprisingly, Newman emphasizes the practical, humanistic, and even social import of a university education. He observes that

> when the Church founds a University, she is *not* cherishing talent, genius, or knowledge, *for their own sake, but for the sake of her children*, with a view to their spiritual welfare and their religious influence and usefulness, with the object of training them to fill their respective posts in life better, and of *making them more intelligent, capable, active members of society*. (p. xxxix; emphasis added)

Assuming that Newman is not simply contradicting himself—"the object of a University is intellectual *not moral*" (emphasis added)—the issue seems to be not if, but *how* the intellectual and moral, the religious and the social, are to be related in a liberal education, which he clearly believes to be fundamentally for the sake of the future Catholic students of a new Catholic university. By way of contrast, "Protestant youths . . . [may] continue their studies till the age of twenty-one or twenty-two; thus they employ a time of life all-important and especially favourable to mental culture. I conceive that our Prelates are impressed with the fact and its consequences, that a [Catholic] youth who ends his education at seventeen is no match (*cÒteris paribus* [everything else being equal]) for one who ends it at twenty-two" (p. xli).

What were the advantages available to Protestant, but not to Catholic, youths in Ireland (and England) in the first half of the nineteenth century and before? It is crucial to hear Newman's answer at some length. Offering almost a *précis* of his main idea, he answers boldly, in a clearly partisan spirit, that what was lacking was

> the culture of the intellect. *Robbed, oppressed, and thrust aside,* Catholics in these islands have not been in a condition for centuries to attempt the sort of education which is necessary for the man of the world, the statesman, the landholder, or the opulent gentleman. Their legitimate stations, duties, employments, have been taken from them, and the qualifications withal, social and intellectual, which are necessary both for reversing the forfeiture and for availing themselves of the reversal. *The time is come when this moral disability must be removed.* Our desideratum is, not the manners and habits of the gentleman . . . but the force, the steadiness, the comprehensiveness and the versatility of intellect, the command over our own powers, the instinctive just estimate of things as they pass before us, which sometimes is a natural gift, but commonly is not gained without much effort and the exercise of years. (p. xliii; emphasis added)

Higher education, according to Cardinal Newman, is for the liberation of the oppressed and for the upward mobility of the robbed, the exploited poor. It is for the inclusion and participation in the mainstream of society of those "thrust aside," the marginalized. A more contemporary-sounding rallying cry (however stilted by contemporary standards of expression it may be) could hardly be imagined.

This liberation is to be accomplished through the cultivation of the intellect that is available only through a university education. The consequent virtues of such cultivation will be force, steadiness, comprehensiveness, versatility, self-command, and good judgment. Elsewhere, Newman extends the list in the same vein to include: "good sense, sobriety of thought, reasonableness, candour" (p. xliii), "freedom, equitableness, calmness, moderation, and wisdom; or what . . . I have ventured to call a philosophical habit [of mind]" (p. 76). In any other context—and that is the context in which Newman's idea of a liberal education is often (mis)understood—these habits of mind would be safe, conventional, taken for granted as desiderata. But when a whole class of citizens has systematically and deliberately been denied them, that is a different story.

For the Sake of the World

But that is not yet the whole story. The benefits of a traditional liberal education—which we now can also name a socially liberating education—extend beyond the student. Knowledge for its own sake, for the sake of the mind of the knower, reaches through the knower to society and world. Contending with those in his day who argued that a classical education was not useful in view of the future material and social advancement of the student, Newman argues for the larger utility of a liberal education because "a great good will impart great good." The great good in question, the cultivation of the intellect, is "useful . . . in a true and high sense . . . to the possessor and to all around him." not "in any low, mechanical, mercantile sense, but as diffusing good, or as a blessing, or a gift, or power, or a treasure, first to the owner, then through him *to the world*" (p. 124; emphasis added).

According to Newman, a university best serves the world not directly but indirectly, by improving people, and by improving people in the manner proper and even unique to a university:

> University training is the great ordinary means to a great ordinary end; it aims at raising the intellectual tone of society, at cultivating the public mind, at purifying the national taste, at supplying true principles to popular enthusiasm and fixed aims to popular aspiration, at giving enlargement and sobriety to the ideas of the age, *at facilitating the exercise of political power*, and refining the intercourse of private life. (p. 134; emphasis added)

Indeed, "why do we educate, except to prepare for the world? Why do we cultivate the intellect of the many beyond the first elements of knowledge, except for this world?" (p. 176). Having joined an historically oppressed minority in his midlife conversion to Catholicism, Newman is supremely aware that this world includes the unjust exercise of political power, and that this injustice can and should be addressed, indirectly but deliberately, through liberal education, to include both those privileged and those marginalized by such injustice.

For Cardinal Newman, "knowledge for its own sake" is only part of the story. His idea of a university also includes, in the first place, the liberation of the oppressed, as he would have understood those terms as a nineteenth-century, socially conservative but politically astute English Catholic; and in the second place, the university as leavening influence in the world, even at its most worldly, in the realm of political power. Had Newman had the intellectual resources of modern CST at his disposal—with its vocabulary of dignity, rights, participation, common good, solidarity, option for the poor, and so forth—would he not have entered them into his understanding of how the Catholic university endeavors to shape the habits of mind and heart of its students? The intrinsic potential for such an explicit integration of the commitment to justice into liberal education is clear.

St. Ignatius Loyola: For the Sake of Others

Three centuries earlier, St. Ignatius, *a fortiori*, also lacked modern CST to guide his "way of proceeding." That has not prevented his Jesuit sons, four centuries later, from speaking of "the commitment to justice in Jesuit higher education."[11] But what was the idea of a university, the educational philosophy, of the founder of what was to become the Catholic Church's first teaching order, who himself became, in effect, Europe's first superintendent of schools?[12]

Iñigo Goes to School

Iñigo of Loyola's (1491–1556) own education as the son of a worldly Basque around the turn of the sixteenth century would have been bare bones.[13] It is, therefore, no small wonder that by the mid–twentieth century, Ignatius[14] could be described as being "as worthy of a place amongst the greatest educators as amongst the saints."[15] How did this transformation of Ignatius' relationship to education take place, and how did the first Father General understand education and its relationship to the newly founded Society of Jesus?

Jesuit historian John O'Malley gives us this lapidary answer: Ignatius, "a few years after his conversion, decided that he needed a university education in order, as he said, 'better to help souls,'"[16] by which Ignatius would have meant "whole persons."[17] In 1526, after two years of the remedial study of Latin with the young boys of Barcelona (p. 9), Ignatius moved on to the University of Alcalá, where he studied logic, physics, and theology (p. 11). But his main academic experience would come at the University of Paris, the leading institution of its kind in that era where, spanning a period of seven years, he pursued the studies that would lead to the Bachelor of Arts, the Licentiate of Arts, and the Master of Arts degrees (pp. 12–15).

Scholasticism versus Humanism

It is much to our purposes to unpack George Ganss' observation that "his seven years of study at Paris" had given Ignatius "a serious introduction to both the scholastic and the humanistic learning of his time" (p. 17). In the 1500s in Europe

> Two institutions were confronting and trying to accommodate each other—the university, a medieval foundation—and the humanistic primary and secondary schools, which began to take shape in fifteenth-century Italy . . . These two institutions were based on fundamentally different, almost opposed, philosophies of education. . . . The universities . . . sprang up in the late twelfth and thirteen centuries largely in response to the recovery in the West of Aristotle's works on logic and what we would today call the sciences. . . . Their goal . . . was the pursuit of truth. Their problem was how to reconcile Christian truth, that is, the Bible, with pagan scientific (or "philosophical") truth, that is, Aristotle.[18]

Even here, "knowledge for its own sake" served a larger purpose, insuring the integrity of the Truth of Revelation.

But the new schools of typically Renaissance mode approached the integrity of Christian life and belief from a more practical perspective and with a different curriculum and aims. The humanistic schools preferred literary over scientific texts, including poetry, drama, oratory, and history. This so-called *studia humanitatis* was pursued for more than eloquence. Indeed, such study was "assumed to inspire noble and uplifting ideals. *They would, if properly taught, render the student a better human being, imbued especially with an ideal of service to the common good,*[19] in imitation of the great heroes of antiquity—an ideal certainly befitting the Christian."[20] In contrast to the universities, "the purpose of this schooling was not so much the pursuit of abstract or speculative truth . . . as the character formation of the student, an ideal the humanists encapsulated in the word *pietas*—not to be translated as piety, though it included it, but as upright character."[21]

The distinguished theologian Michael J. Buckley, S.J., remarks on this historical shift in more contemporary terms: "The 'abstract' medieval arts gave way to the concrete humanities, and this focus upon particularity embodied a new orientation towards social action and efficacy and a conjunction between literary education and moral and religious formation."[22]

Pietas as *Christianitas*

But what did the Society itself bring to this somewhat contentious mix? As Buckley points out, "Jesuit higher education does not come out of a prior philosophy of education. It comes out of a spirituality."[23] From the Spiritual Exercises, the companions took what O'Malley calls "an impulse to interiority,"[24] which had influenced their teaching of catechism before they began opening schools. That basic instruction in Christian belief and conduct included not only "the Apostles Creed, the Ten Commandments, and basic prayers, but also . . . the so-called spiritual and corporal works of mercy—feeding the hungry, clothing the naked, welcoming the stranger. These were ultimately derived from the 25th chapter of Matthew's Gospel, where Jesus said that to do these things for the needy was to do them to *Him*."[25]

This "art of Christian living," known at the time as *Christianitas*, correlated well with the *pietas* of the Renaissance humanists, and thus became a defining element of the mission of the Society's schools.[26] That explains the deep religious motivation for the policy that Ignatius insisted upon: that Jesuit schools be endowed sufficiently so that no tuition need be charged and the poor not excluded from them. As O'Malley reports, one of the rationales for the schools was "that poor boys, who could not possibly pay for teachers, much less for private tutors, will make progress in learning and that their parents will be able to satisfy their obligation to educate their children." The expected contribution of the schools to the common good could not be stated any more clearly: "'Those who are now only students will grow up to be pastors, civic officials, administrators of justice, and will fill other important posts to everybody's profit and advantage.'"[27] O'Malley further remarks that "while the Jesuits of course had no idea of what we today call 'upward social mobility,' the schools in fact acted in some instances as an opportunity for precisely that."[28] Thus, in this very early Ignatian model, we see both a commitment to educate the poor (no tuition) and the nonpoor on behalf of the poor,[29] or to what I have previously described as the twofold nature of education for justice.

Ignatius' Idea of a Jesuit University: The Best of Both Worlds

But how did these early Jesuits—all ten of the original company were educated at the University of Paris—reconcile the medieval scholastic pursuit of truth and the Renaissance humanist pursuit of personal and social betterment? Perhaps that opposition is softened if we remember that for the medieval scholars, the pursuit of truth ultimately served Christian revelation and that Renaissance humanists, such as the members of the Society of Jesus,[30] were deeply committed Christians who understood *pietas* in light of *Christianitas*. That answers the reconciliation question in a way intrinsic to the Christian worldview, but there's another more practical response.

Although Ignatius, during his 15-year tenure as head of the Jesuits, gave approval to some 40 school foundations, only one of them (the Roman College, later known as the Gregorian University) would be recognized today as resembling a university, the rest being closer to our secondary schools. So it is at first a bit of a puzzle why George Ganss titled his magisterial work *Saint Ignatius' Idea of a Jesuit University*. In fact, he remarks that it might well have been named "St. *Ignatius' Ideas on Education* or *Saint Ignatius' Concept of Christian Paideia*."[31] But his "Schematic Outline: A University as Conceived by St. Ignatius"[32] goes a long way toward solving that puzzle. The outline traces pupils from ages 5 to 23 and divides their studies into the modern elementary, secondary, and higher categories. The Society enters the picture during the secondary years, from 10 to 13, through instruction in humane letters. Higher education, from years 14 to 23, is devoted first to philosophy (logic, physics, metaphysics, moral science, mathematics) and second to theology, law, or medicine (what we would call graduate or professional school).

For Ignatius, what we would call high school (and even junior high or middle school) is included in the university, whereas we would reserve that term for post-secondary education. That is, in Ignatius' idea of a university, the medieval scholastic and the renaissance humanistic philosophies and institutions of education are both honored and indeed integrated into a single vision of the educated person from childhood to young adulthood (although not all students would have gone on to study law, medicine, or theology).

Finally, and most importantly for our purposes, is Ignatius' understanding of the mission of such an educational institution. He himself pursued a university education in order "better to help souls." He eventually came to understand that the best way for the Society to help souls was also through education[33] and that the purpose of that education was to "render the student a better human being, imbued especially with an ideal of service to the common good, in imitation of the great heroes of antiquity—an ideal certainly befitting the Christian."[34]

Justice Education and the Contemporary Catholic University

I have argued that both Newman and Ignatius had a profound understanding of the moral and social dimensions of a Catholic university education and articulated and implemented that understanding in ways appropriate to their cultural and historical contexts. Newman and Ignatius thus provide a solid historical and intellectual foundation on which to build an explicitly modern view of a socially engaged Catholic university education.

In August 1990, Pope John Paul II issued the Apostolic Constitution, *Ex Corde Ecclesiae*[35] (*From the Heart of the Church*). Its status as the governing document for Catholic universities worldwide meant that most of the ensuing attention, at least in the United States, was paid to the relationship between the required episcopal *mandatum* for Catholic theologians, and academic freedom and civil law. Unfortunately, that has meant that the substance of the document has often been overlooked. The Pope could hardly be any more explicit about the theme of this chapter: "The Christian spirit of service to others for the *promotion of social justice* is of particular importance for each Catholic university, to be shared by its teachers and developed in its students" (§34; emphasis in original). He does not elaborate on *how* in particular this teaching and learning is to be accomplished, but the Pope does argue that a Catholic university education should be made "accessible to all those who are able to benefit from it, especially the poor or members of minority groups who customarily have been deprived of it" (§34). But he also puts this imperative, which we saw in Newman and Ignatius, in global perspective: "A Catholic university also has the responsibility, to the degree that it is able, to help to promote the development of the emerging nations" (§34). In short, Catholic universities "are committed to the promotion of solidarity and its meaning in society *and in the world*" (§37; emphasis added).

On the occasion of the inauguration of a president at Spring Hill College on the day before the beginning of Holy Week in 1990, the same year that *Ex Corde* appeared, Michael J. Buckley, S.J., offered a profound meditation on "Education Marked with the Sign of the Cross." He notes that for Ignatius the passion of Christ was "a twofold experience . . . of the absence of God . . . and . . . of an enormity of human suffering." This Ignatian insight about the Passion suggests "the two major challenges of Jesuit education within the United States today: the massive absence of God from so much of the contemporary world . . . [and] the suffering of humanity—with all the wretchedness of the four million homeless in our major cities and the refugees at our border, impoverished families, boat people and the starving in Africa, the exploited and the tortured."[36] "Educate our students 'comfortably,'" continues Buckley, "without the sensibility, the awareness, the reflective skills, and the desire to confront these two dimensions of human existence . . . and you have not given them a Catholic education adequate for our time."[37]

Buckley then asked his audience to remember the previous November 16, when six Jesuits at the University of Central America (UCA) in El Salvador were assassinated because of their commitment to justice for the poor majority of Salvadorans. He observed that "what happened in El Salvador to these men is not so much a barbarous and bizarre anomaly as, somehow or other, a sacramental sign lifted up of what our higher education must always be about." Although Buckley speaks with a particularly Ignatian accent, what he says holds true for all Catholic colleges and universities: "Higher education is neither propaganda nor indoctrination. But Catholic and Jesuit higher education must also educate its students into the disciplined sensitivity toward the suffering in the world."[38] Otherwise, our students will graduate "underdeveloped religiously and humanistically because ignorantly indifferent to what is the lot of the great majority of human beings."[39]

According to the martyred rector of the UCA, Ignacio Ellacuría, S.J., this could be true even in El Salvador because "any university student here is privileged and should be held accountable as a privileged person."[40] Thus, Ellacuría narrowed any sort of gap between the two types of justice education we have identified: In his estimation, higher education of the poor necessarily *becomes* education of the privileged—just as education of the privileged becomes education on behalf of the marginalized. In terms of the university's mission, the important point about the character of the student body is not so much *where they come from* (the impoverished *campo*, the alienated ghetto, the isolated reservation, or the affluent suburbs) but *where they are going*[41] (into careers of personal advancement only or into vocations rooted in a human solidarity that knows no bounds).

This emphasis on student development, transformation, and vocation by both Ellacuría (1975) and Buckley (1990) is a precursor to the oft-quoted dictum of Fr. Peter-Hans Kolvenbach, S.J., (2000) that "the measure of Jesuit universities is not what our students do but who they become and the adult Christian responsibility they will exercise in future towards their neighbor and their world."[42] In Buckley's words, the "challenge of the Christian cross to . . . education [is] to become increasingly part of these enormous struggles, patterned on those of the passion of Christ."[43] To educate students for or into the struggle for global justice, in other words, is a powerful way to bring both young people, whether rich or poor, and their mentors into deeper solidarity with Christ himself.

From Ignatius to Newman to their contemporary heirs, each in his own historical and social context, education for justice is conceived of as constitutive of Catholic higher education. The focus on education for justice in the contemporary Catholic university is no innovation at all, however it may be shaped by modern Catholic social teaching and a globalized social reality. Although presentation of a fully fledged pedagogy of justice according to that body of teaching is presented in the following chapter, it may be helpful to outline some educational practices responsive to this vision.

Contemporary Examples of Education for Justice

As Catholic and Jesuit, Creighton University (CU) is affiliated with the Wisconsin Province of the Society of Jesus, which has sponsored ministries on the Pine Ridge and Rosebud Lakota Indian reservations in western South Dakota for many decades. In recent years, the University, located in Omaha, Nebraska, has made special efforts to recruit, retain, and graduate young people from those communities that are located in some of the poorest counties in the United States, and where rates of unemployment, school drop-out, diabetes, and alcoholism are among the highest in the country. For several years, Creighton has sponsored a retreat for Native American high school students from these reservations and throughout the country with the purpose of encouraging them to pursue higher education and providing them with the guidance to do so. Employees of the University have volunteered to serve as mentors for some of these students as they apply for Gates Millennium Scholars awards and other grants. The only Native American Studies program at a Jesuit university offers both a major and a minor and has been developed, in part, to provide a curriculum of special relevance to Native American students. An "All Nations Pow-Wow" has been hosted on the campus to celebrate Native culture and peoples for the edification and enjoyment of the wider University community. And recently a special section of the Ratio Studiorum Program, Creighton's first-year experience, has been created for Indian students and is led by a nationally respected Indian educator and former tribal chairman.

But what about those students from the affluent suburbs of Omaha, Minneapolis, Chicago, or Denver, or those students from smaller towns in Nebraska and Iowa whose parents are themselves successful professionals? Many of these students are drawn to Creighton because a CU undergraduate degree is seen as a ticket to one of CU's several professional schools in the health sciences. As reported in Chapter 4, since 1992, Creighton has offered a study abroad experience in the Dominican Republic.[44] For a full semester, as many as 19 students are immersed in another culture, speak another language, live in close and intentional community on a small campus where health outreach programs for the rural poor are also housed, enjoy the generous hospitality of Dominican or Haitian-Dominican families in remote mountain villages or isolated migrant worker communities, volunteer in schools and health care facilities and other programs serving the poor, work on community development projects such as a water system or bridge—all the while taking a slate of courses especially designed for the context, and while participating in regular reflection and retreats. Upon their return to campus, many of these students take courses in the Justice and Peace Studies Program (established in 1995), which now offers both a major and a minor, and through which they and other service-inspired students study Catholic social teaching, moral exemplars such as Archbishop Romero and Mahatma Gandhi (see Chapter 6), Christian ethics of war and peace, methods of social analysis, strategies for pursuing social justice, and skills of vocational discernment.

Although these innovative and intensive efforts on behalf of education for justice in its twofold nature reach a relatively small number of students at one university, they do provide representative and substantial evidence that this constitutive dimension of the tradition of Catholic higher education, as developed by Saint Ignatius and his followers and as articulated by Cardinal Newman, is thriving in the heart of the American Catholic Church today. Were they able to observe these efforts, I believe those two giants of Catholic higher education would approve.

My thesis in this chapter has been that the educational models developed by Saint Ignatius of Loyola, founder of the Society of Jesus, and John Henry Cardinal Newman, author of the classic *The Idea of a University*, two major sources from the deep tradition of Catholic higher education, demonstrate that concern for what we now call social justice has long been a fundamental dimension of the Catholic university in its relationship to its students, and who those students are and are becoming, as a matter of intellectual, moral, and spiritual formation. I have also pointed out that in his apostolic constitution of the Catholic university, Pope John Paul II endorsed and extended this vision to address contemporary global realities. He did so, of course, in the context of a century of modern Catholic social teaching, to which he himself contributed substantially. Education for justice, of both the privileged and the marginalized, is indeed *constitutive* of the mission of the Catholic university.

The following concluding chapter recapitulates and weaves together the major themes of the preceding seven chapters, especially in light of the major influence of Aristotle and Ignatius. Chapter 8 probes more deeply the pedagogical implications of the student experience of shame that often arises in personal encounter with the poor and marginalized, whether through service-learning courses or immersion programs, or as might arise also in imaginative encounter with moral exemplars in the classroom. It offers a practical example of how the three justice pedagogies examined in Part II have been integrated into the Pedagogical Circle in one undergraduate program. Some of the students who have participated in this program are given the chance to speak for themselves. Finally, I offer some concluding thoughts on young adult vocational development in Catholic higher education.

8 Aristotle, Ignatius, and the Painful Path to Solidarity

A Pedagogy for Justice in Catholic Higher Education

> There are truths that can only be discovered through suffering or from the critical vantage point of extreme situations.
>
> *Ignacio Martín-Baro*, S.J.[1]

This final chapter has five purposes: (1) In keeping with the pedagogical practice of repetition, I highlight in narrative fashion the principle images, arguments, insights, and discoveries of the preceding chapters; (2) I bear down more deeply into the question of shame, in both its unhealthy and healthy forms, a perhaps surprising theme in a book on justice education within formal academic settings; (3) I outline how these pedagogical ideas get played out and come together in the undergraduate program I have designed and direct; (4) I offer several especially compelling excerpts from student writing; and (5) I suggest 11 theses on young adult vocational development in the context of Catholic higher education. We will look back, we will look deeper, we will look at a model, we will listen, and we will draw some brief conclusions. First, what have we learned? I answer that question in three subsections: on discovering a pattern of personal encounter with the poor and marginalized, on the crossing of social borders and the discovery of one's privileged social location, and on how Catholic higher education has incorporated some of these themes in two major historical expressions.

A Narrative and Thematic Review

Discovering a Pattern

The deep origins of this book can be traced to my personal encounter with the poor of Tijuana, Mexico, three decades ago, before I had any thought of being a professor of Justice and Peace Studies in a Catholic university. For three years in the early 1980s, my monthly trek from the affluence and opulence of Santa Barbara to Tijuana, the tip of the Two-Thirds World (see Chapter 1), was a profoundly unsettling and formative experience. Some years later, I resonated with the not dissimilar experience of Mev Puleo, who, as a young teenager vacationing with her family in Brazil, suffered a crisis of conscience, at least in germ, as their tourist bus made its way toward the magnificent statue of Christ overlooking both the misery and luxury of Rio de Janeiro. I took as my own the "cry of anguish" of the globetrotting Pope Paul VI, in *Populorum Progressio*, as he, not unlike Mev in her young adult years, tried to narrow the gap between the rich North (the developed nations) and the poor South (the underdeveloped or developing nations). Over those early years, I came to see such experiences, both my own and those of others, as forming a pattern of encounter, crisis, and commitment.

So I was not surprised to discover more recently that Fr. Pedro Arrupe, S.J., under whose courageous post–Vatican II leadership, the Society of Jesus made justice an essential dimension of its mission, had experienced his own formative crisis of conscience as a young medical student in Madrid when he encountered the suffering poor, and thereby his own privilege, in a world of sin and injustice. And once again I was consoled to find in Catholic social teaching (CST) a reflection of my own experiences, when I discovered the compact argument in *Justitia in Mundo* (*Justice in the World*) that education for justice requires "a renewal of the heart, based on the recognition of sin in its individual and social manifestations," especially "through action, participation, and vital contact with the reality of injustice" (see Chapter 2).

No one has spelled out this insight more succinctly and eloquently than Fr. Peter-Hans Kolvenbach, S.J., Arrupe's successor as Superior-General of the Society of Jesus at the time of his watershed address at Santa Clara University in 2000: College students need "personal involvement with innocent suffering, with the injustices others suffer" so that they can "let the gritty reality of this world into their lives, so they can learn to feel it, think about it critically, respond to its suffering, and engage it constructively." Or, as Fr. Kolvenbach summed up the mission of the intellectual apostolate: "The real measure of our Jesuit universities lies in who our students become" (see Chapter 2). I would amend that to include all Catholic higher education. To that essential pattern of encounter, crisis, and commitment, we can add the language and practice of insertion or immersion in marginalized communities, empathy, social analysis, theological and ethical reflection, and vocational discernment—or, as I have called it, the Pedagogical Circle.

Crossing Borders

I have learned that education for justice is all about the intimately personal risk that accompanies crossing borders—national, geographical, cultural, class—and thereby discovering one's privileged social location in a world of destitution.[2] As my students say, it's about getting out of your comfort zone. What some of them also acknowledge, more importantly, is that leaving your comfort zone means getting into a *discomfort* zone, such as a homeless shelter just blocks from your campus suite, or the site of a massacre of Salvadoran peasants made possible by U.S. tax dollars and U.S. foreign policy. Being formed for justice, undergoing a conversion to the cause of the poor, can be—perhaps must be—if not wholly, still crucially, a painful experience.

Researching this book has led me to a heightened appreciation of the role of what St. Ignatius inferred was the *grace* of shame and confusion in the process of personal conversion, which is so central to (if not synonymous with) education for justice. In attending to the experiences of students in *Semestre Dominicano*, I saw tears and heard expressions of moral anguish. "It hurts to be compassionate" when compassion provides no easy fix to oppression in the lives of people who have cared for you as for family. Even worse, as a young and naïve First-Worlder, not only may you be unable to contribute very much if anything to solving the problems of the poor, but in your previously unexamined privilege, you may be part of the problem. "Go home, you're not needed" (Ian Illich) are "piercing words" (a student's response to Illich; see Chapter 3). Such encounters can lead to the cognitive disequilibration and personal crisis necessary for the construction of a moral rationality that transcends social convention. When teamed with an openness to personal vulnerability, a radical change of environment—such as what an immersion trip represents, with its accompanying risk—can provoke empathic distress and guilt over affluence, which can present just the disorienting dilemma necessary to provoke a process of personal transformation.

But one need not travel to distant lands to have such an experience with its attendant difficult emotions. The testimonies of students participating in domestic service-learning programs for justice report similar feelings, similar stumblings. As one scholar reported of one such program, "the shock stage of service-learning is important because it provides a sharp emotional and psychological jolt to students' perceptions of reality."[3] That shock may encompass a range of affective states: discomfort, anxiety, sadness, pity, guilt, anger, humiliation, and shame. Such states may go deep and rattle the bones, as one student expressed it, or seem to erupt from one's gut, in another student's language. In some cases at least, the pain of privilege meeting poverty is visceral. It's all about discovering who we are and where we are, relative to the pain of other people's lives, a pain of which we had previously been blissfully unaware, and which now almost mocks us with its stare. It's as if, said one student who had visited a homeless shelter, we were "magnets of resentment." One can almost hear the subtext of this encounter: *But I'm a good person, I'm here to help! Please don't judge me!*

But one need not leave campus to be challenged by the reality of other people's lives. The study of moral exemplars can also expand students' sense of the human condition and what is possible within it. In this case, however, the reality revealed is not the depths to which human misery can sink but the heights to which human virtue can climb in response to that very misery. Drawing on what has been said of saints as liminal figures, we can infer that moral exemplars are also both paradigmatic and prophetic figures. They embody social norms but also transcend them; and in their transcendent loyalties, values, and integrity, may pose a trenchant critique to and of anyone willing to take them seriously. Emulation of such luminaries, we learn from Aristotle, is a good feeling felt by good persons. But good does not mean pleasant. In fact, emulation is a distressing or painful emotion expressing my realization that I lack some human good that I admire in others. When I falter in my pursuit of such a good or goods, though—when I discover myself not to be as virtuous as I had previously thought—I may experience the semi-virtue of shame, another painful, but potentially motivating, emotion.

According to Aristotle, the "grandfather of service-learning," such experiences of emulation and shame are most likely to happen in the young, whose lofty aspirations and noble dispositions make them vulnerable to emulation but whose fickleness and instability of character also make them vulnerable to shame. Perhaps intuiting such struggles, the young may admire, from a distance, the merciful and heroic deeds of a figure like Dorothy Day but resist her explicit call, echoing Jesus, to go and do likewise, to emulate the saints, especially the saints of a new social order. In the face of the imperative or duty to become better persons, and then even-better persons, doing today what we could not have done yesterday, not just young adults in seminar settings on privileged campuses but their older mentors may dismiss the saints too easily. If Nietzsche is right, it's a deep challenge to love oneself enough to contemn the self we are now and embrace the higher self that we could become. Still, I'm often inspired by the degree to which my own students do indeed acknowledge and accept that challenge, in which case they become moral exemplars to me.

Social Location and Community Practice

The painful emotions are only where we begin, in education for justice, not where we stay or end although we may never escape them entirely. Certainly Aristotle had much more to say about human flourishing or happiness than that the path to such *eudaimonia* (human flourishing or happiness) is sometimes, even necessarily, painful. Seeing the misery or the nobility of others may prompt a daunting self-examination, but seeing the world as it is constitutes only the first step in responding authentically to it. We have traced the "see-judge-act" dynamic of Catholic Social Action and of Catholic Social Teaching to Aristotle's *phronesis*, or practical reason. The well-known Pastoral Circle, as developed by Holland and Henriot from see-judge-act, adds Insertion or awareness of social location to that three-part dynamic. By substituting Vocational Discernment for Pastoral Planning, we transformed the Pastoral Circle into the Pedagogical Circle, and we have seen how that accords with the long and distinguished history of Ignatian spirituality and pedagogy (as encapsulated by Fr. Kolvenbach at Santa Clara), both grounded in intimate personal experience and imagination. In the last few decades, Ignatian spirituality and pedagogy have embraced the promotion of justice as an absolute requirement, explicitly in Jesuit institutions and on their own terms in many other Catholic colleges and universities.

But social location might also mean community practice. We have argued that MacIntyre's analysis of the possibility of genuine and determinate virtue as requiring communities of ethical tradition, practice, and inquiry points up the inestimable value of Catholic Social Action and Teaching as the obvious and only contexts in which Catholic Social Virtue can be taught. We have demonstrated that such educational practices actually predate the late–nineteenth-century development of the modern teaching of the Church on social issues. The schools of the Society of Jesus, from the earliest instances in the sixteenth century, embodied what we would call today the preferential option for the poor, solidarity beyond class, and practical commitment to the common good. Those schools, bringing together the Medieval university's search for truth and the Renaissance school's formation in Christian humanism, practiced education *of* the poor for their advancement *and* education of the rich not only for their entry intro the professions but also *on behalf of* the poor, for the good of the community as a whole.

Catholic universities today, when they make similar commitments, far from being innovative or even betraying some vaunted academic ideal of knowledge for its own sake, of a deracinated and elite life of the mind, are simply updating a deep historical tradition. Knowledge for its own sake, we discovered in a close reading of Newman, is knowledge for the sake of the learner, especially when that learner belongs to a marginalized and exploited class, and thereby knowledge for the sake of the world, for its betterment, for its greater justice. Along with all the necessary paracurricular programs that create a fertile and supportive context on our campuses, justice and peace studies programs in Catholic colleges and universities (by whatever names they are called), when faithful to their heritage (both centuries distant and as contemporary as the most recent social encyclical), may be counted as communities of resistance to injustice (in MacIntyre's language; see Chapter 3) or as Abrahamic minorities (in the phrase used by Archbishop Dom Helder Camara, one of the prime movers at Vatican II and in the progressive Latin American Church).[4] They are leaven within Catholic institutions of higher education, urging them to live up to their own mission statements, just as Catholic higher education ought to be intellectual leaven within the Church, even as the Church endeavors to leaven society.

But is the experience of shame, as I have contended, really a necessary and even inevitable dimension of that leavening action? I'll have more to say about that in a moment, but lest there be any resistance to the positive role that shame has to play in personal conversion and education for justice, it is important to acknowledge the ways in which some forms of shame can be negative and opposed to human flourishing and social justice. I presume that similar arguments can be made for the other painful emotions (anger, for example), but I will not attempt to do so here. Psychologist/theologian James W. Fowler, known especially for his theory of faith development,[5] provides an exacting analysis of both good and bad forms of shame.

Shame as Grace and Disgrace

When Shame Is Not a Grace

Fowler offers a spectrum of shame.[6] At one end of the spectrum, we find healthy shame in two forms. *Discretionary shame* "protects those qualities of personhood that are grounds for esteem in the eyes of others and for honest confidence and pride in the self," is "premonitory and anticipatory," and depends upon the moral imagination to foresee how possible actions might play out (p. 105). *Disgrace shame*, on the other hand, is not anterior but posterior to a revealing act and "evolves as the painful set of emotions in which one feels exposed as unworthy, as defective, or as having failed to meet some set of standards necessary for the esteem of important others and of the self" (p. 105). Disgrace shame is more global than guilt, just as the pattern or trajectory of a life is distinguished from one action within that life. In both of these healthy forms, shame, as "the caretaker of our worthy selves and identities," provides a foundation for conscience (p. 92). In many of the accounts of student experiences that I have examined, disgrace shame is clearly at work. One of the primary tasks of Catholic social learning, as for Catholic education generally, is the fostering of healthy shame—or, as we are more likely to say, the formation of conscience.

These two forms of healthy shame are both nicely demonstrated in this student reflection on her experience volunteering at a nursing home for the elderly as part of a service-learning course:

> At the nursing home I feel very uncomfortable every time I go. I get a sick feeling in my stomach that does not leave until I go home. The residents are so sick, both mentally and physically, it scares me. But, at the same time, I am beginning to understand why Jesus taught the message that he taught. The world that I live in has always been filled with love and security. I have my share of problems, but nothing world shattering. Being at the nursing home helps me to realize that not everyone lives the life I do. It also has helped me to realize that maybe I am not as nice, caring, and religious as I have always supposed I am. Jesus taught his message to help the poor get a good night's sleep and to help the rich wake up.
>
> The other day I saw a man in his forties sitting outside the nursing home. He looked shabby and very rough. All I could think was to wonder why this man was standing around bothering the residents. He made me nervous. Then one of the residents called out to him with a big grin, and the man grinned back. I found out that the man is a construction worker in the area who comes to volunteer during his lunch hour and after work.

> The only other volunteer I have met at the home is a man named Donny, who I thought was a resident the first time I saw him. Donny does not look older than forty-five but is in a wheelchair and speaks slowly. There is something wrong with him physically. He volunteers more than twenty hours a week, and the residents know him by heart and love him. I am beginning to feel very ashamed of myself. Not only do I judge the residents, but the other volunteers. While I am doing this they are helping each other attempt to live a better, more fulfilled life. As sick as I feel when I think of going, I am beginning to feel even worse at the idea of not going.

This honest and painful self-assessment expresses both disgrace shame—"I am beginning to feel very ashamed of myself"—and discretionary shame—"I am beginning to feel even worse at the idea of not going." The dynamic is fascinating. Because she is aware of being ashamed of her present attitudes, she can foresee that acting to avoid them in the future, by not returning to the site that provokes those attitudes and that shame, would cause an even more disturbing shame. What kind of person is she? It would be cowardly and niggardly and selfish, she seems to imagine, to abandon people who themselves rise above the very impairments that scare her or whose appearance makes her nervous but whose generosity of self seems to accuse her. Whether one thinks of this as semivirtuous or healthy shame, surely it is to be applauded and encouraged, even as one commiserates and even identifies with her in her painful self-revelation.

A very different kind of shame—*perfectionist shame*, often with roots in early childhood—is distorting and unhealthy. In thrall to the approval of important others, who may seem never to be satisfied, perfectionist shame limits access to the truth of one's own experience and self-evaluation (p. 114). Whereas healthy shame nurtures or protects a true self-identity, perfectionist shame creates a false self-identity, which is "reinforced by the parents, with the sanctions of religious and class ideals of moral superiority" (p. 115). Scruples, to which Ignatius was prone early in his conversion experience,[7] would seem to be a version of perfectionist shame in which one becomes one's own worst enemy. This inflated form of shame lacks humility and compassion toward the self; conviction about the enormity of one's own sins makes forgiveness impossible.

Ascribed shame, or "shame due to enforced minority status," is another story altogether. It can be learned within a family of marginalized social status even before the child is exposed to the wider world. "It has little to do with the personal qualities of the family or their children. It has everything to do with the social environment's disvaluing of some qualities over which they have no control. Most potent among the forms of this type of ascribed shame are the distortions due to socioeconomic class, race, ethnic background, sometimes religion, and—most commonly—gender" (p. 119). Two factors make this shame especially pernicious and difficult: it can exist alongside any of the other forms of shame on the spectrum, and it cannot be fully healed apart from addressing issues of social justice. So the healthy shame that privileged students might feel in a homeless shelter may be complicated by an awareness of the ascribed shame—the socially unjust shame—that they see in the shelter's guests. One such student seems to have been angered, shamed, and motivated by the way her older affluent peers (ladies of the Junior League) condescended to the women of the shelter and thereby reinforced their ascribed shame.[8]

In *Volunteer with the Poor in Peru*, Jeff Thielman reports on his three-year stint as a recent Boston College graduate trying to make a difference in the lives of poor children in the city of Tacna. Soon after arriving at his new residence at a Jesuit high school, where he was to teach and coach, Jeff took his "first undistracted look at where I was":

> Somehow I had not noticed how dramatically the barbed wire fence separated our lovely property from the poor neighborhood almost in our back yard which, in my home town, would be considered a slum. A woman who had brought her plastic water bucket to an outdoor spigot suddenly straightened up, cocked her head, put her hands on her hips, and stared at me directly. Her children, in torn, dirty clothing, with dusty hands and feet, stared at me too—as my gold Seiko watch and my gold college ring, in my imagination, took on an enormous weight and proportion on my wrist and finger. Both were gifts; but the ring now became emblematic

> not so much of me as a person—as if Boston College had given me my identity—but of the world I had left behind. For a passing second the woman's eyes and mine met. Perhaps she was embarrassed as I.[9]

A student who had participated in *Semestre Dominicano* commented on this passage, read for a course upon her return to Omaha, that both the poor woman and the rich volunteer "feel that there is something shameful in the way they live," and that "there is something about seeing the stark contrast between your own world and somebody else's that is incredibly powerful." We might also say that there is something powerful about the encounter between unjustly ascribed shame for poverty and healthy shame for previously unacknowledged privilege.

Toxic shame arises in children whose families are dysfunctionally organized around a parent's alcoholism or abusiveness. A false self must be constantly on display or at hand, playing by the rules that allow the dysfunction to remain publicly unchallenged and the alcoholic or abuser unaccountable for his behavior. The suppression of the true self's suffering becomes poisonous. As toxic shame may often be present among the poor and marginalized, as both cause and consequence of their plight, our students may often encounter it hidden in the resentment of those they expect to find appreciative of their presence and service.

Finally, at the far end of the spectrum from healthy shame is *shamelessness*, or *sociopathology*: the complete lack of empathy, respect, and conscience. Fowler gives as examples the political tyrants Stalin, Hitler, and Saddam Hussein, each of whose biographies reveal childhoods in which abusive or shut-off parents made the development of healthy shame an impossibility.

I conclude that the distance between virtue and vice, between sanctity and villainy, is measured by the kinds of shame active in any particular person. Healthy shame keeps us human and humane and nurtures holiness; unhealthy shame suppresses our own deepest humanity and that of others; the black hole of a life without shame may suck entire peoples into its destructive maw. The stakes could not be higher. No wonder shame and confusion play an essential role in Christian spirituality.

The Painful Path to Solidarity: "Sunday Mornin' Comin' Down"

Dr. King pointed out that Sunday at eleven o'clock was the most segregated hour of the week in Christian America. Sunday morning was meant to be a time of revelation or of remembering revelation, but what Dr. King revealed to us was the irony of how that revelation itself was undermined by the social locations in which it was practiced. Sunday morning has a way of being a moment of uncomfortable truth.

One of the classic pop-cultural expressions of that reality is singer/songwriter Kris Kristofferson's lament "Sunday Mornin' Comin' Down."[10] The chorus, even minus the rest of the imagery and the music, gives some idea of the self-revelation the narrator is confronting:

> On the Sunday mornin' sidewalk,
> Wishing, Lord, that I was stoned.
> Cause there's somethin' in a Sunday,
> Makes a body feel alone.
> And there's nothin' short of dyin',
> Half as lonesome as the sound,
> On the sleepin' city sidewalks:
> Sunday mornin' comin' down.

In a Christian cultural context, there's nothing like a lonely Sunday morning to reveal the loss of relationship, community, dreams, and faith.

Rev. King suggested that Sunday morning should be a time of stock-taking of their social witness for the Christian churches of America. For Kristofferson, the stock-taking is also spiritual but much more intimate. In both cases, the Sunday morning revelation is bleak, and, of course, ironically so.[11]

In recent years, it has been my wife's and my practice to attend mass at 4:30 Sunday afternoon. That leaves Sunday morning free for a leisurely coffee on the porch while reading *The New York Times* and the local newspaper. Over a period of some weeks, I began to notice that by mid-morning, I was finding myself in a bit of a funk. So much bad news. So much contention, strife, suffering, scandal, betrayal, abuse, injustice, violence, war, even genocide. After a few weeks of this, it finally dawned on me to put my funk in the context not just of Sunday mornin' comin' down, but of the Sabbath, of the Gospel, and more specifically, of the Ignatian Spiritual Exercises. I remembered how Ignatius, in the first "week" or stage of the retreat, instructs the retreatant to take a God's eye view of the human condition, of its endless cycle of sin and suffering and death. That sin, I knew, was both personal and social. At the very least, I was guilty of the sin of omission. I had done so much that made such little difference. And whatever I did this coming week, the news would be just as bad next Sunday morning. Moreover, I was guilty of the sin of complicity, of refusing to refuse to cooperate with evil—of being, in Thomas Merton's memorable phrase, a guilty bystander. I was very much the human in the human condition. No one can do enough, and no one is pure before the sin of the world. No one of any moral and spiritual sensitivity, I suspect, is immune to this kind of funk.

But I also remembered Ignatius' insistence, in the preliminary Principle and Foundation, that Creation is good, even with its human corruption, and that we ourselves have been created by God out of a love that sustains and redeems. But how do we get in touch with that love and how does that redemption happen? I remembered what has become for me the salient insight of the Exercises: the appropriate human response to all that funk-inducing bad news is "shame and confusion." Indeed, Ignatius writes that the retreatant "must *beg* for shame and confusion."[12] What could be more counterintuitive? The Sunday-morning-bad-news-blues comin' down on me could be a gift, a *grace*, even though I have not begged for it and even wished it would go away. If I were to allow myself really to *feel and understand*[13] this interior movement—rather than fight it or repress it or ignore it—it could become precious interior knowledge, and that knowledge could go deep, touching into an essential goodness that was, somehow, Jesus himself. Jesus wept over the suffering of his people, especially the poor and oppressed (the bad news of his day), tried to do something about it, called others to do likewise, suffered the resistance of the Powers That Be,[14] was brutally killed, but proved eternally resilient.

My own tears, whether actual or not on any particular Sunday morning, were a kind of baptism into this familiar pattern of the Exercises, and through them into the dynamics of encounter with Jesus and his Gospel. My shame and confusion were an invitation to forgiveness, liberation, empowerment. The news the next Sunday might not be different, but people all over the world—some inspired by Jesus and some not; many of the poor themselves; some of the rich; and not a few middling persons like myself, exemplars and stamp-lickers, organized in all sorts of ways—were going to try to make a difference, and would sometimes succeed, on occasion, magnificently so. It was worth the effort, even if there were no guarantees. It was the call of grace.

So I have come to be neither surprised nor disheartened when students I know or read about report painful emotions when they encounter the sin of the world, and their share in it, whether they call it that or not, and whether or not they identify their response as the grace of shame and confusion. Indeed, my concern would be raised if they did *not* experience some difficult emotions. The gritty reality of the world is like that. It raises excruciating questions, both personal and social. In the appropriate context of a community of faith and resistance, of an Abrahamic minority, and with proper guidance, such emotions can lead to the kind of self-knowledge and vocational discernment that is an essential dimension of the Catholic university's mission on behalf of its students. It is the context in which all the professions for which we prepare our students make ultimate sense and from which they take their deepest meaning.

Shame in this context can be not only psychologically healthy, but also fundamental to human development (as argued by Fowler), not only a semi-virtue (as named by Aristotle), but also a grace (as prayed for by Ignatius): a path to solidarity and a door to the sacred.

A Model of Justice Pedagogy in Catholic Higher Education

But what does all this look like in practical terms? How do immersion experiences, service-learning courses, and the study of moral exemplars come together in one curriculum? What else is required to create an academic context in which the insights we have gleaned from personal experience, from Aristotle, Ignatius, Newman, MacIntyre, Hoffman, Kolvenbach, Flescher, and CST itself, can be made concrete in a justice education program at a Catholic university? I have no illusion that there is no other effective way to foster Catholic social learning in higher education, but I am confident that the model I have developed over the past 15 years is one such way. Although the fundamental insight—that personal encounter with victims of social injustice is the indispensable first step in education for justice—antedates this program, many of the others have been developed as I have reflected on my teaching experience and the learning experience of my students.[15]

The Justice and Peace Studies (JPS) minor comprises six requirements totaling 18 credit hours, as do all minors in the Creighton University College of Arts & Sciences. These are generally upper-division undergraduate courses.

1. *A service-learning course.* Many JPS students meet this requirement by completing JPS 361 *Social Justice in the Dominican Republic* as participants in *Encuentro Dominicano*,[16] Creighton's study/immersion/service semester program in that Caribbean nation. Others participate in JPS 341 *Ecclesiology in Context: The Church in El Salvador*, a summer travel course.[17] JPS 470 *Poverty in America* is also a summer travel course, but in this case to an Appalachian community in West Virginia. JPS 465 *Faith and Political Action* is offered as a local service-learning course. Whether local, national, or international, all these courses engage students in marginalized communities and their concerns. (See Chapters 4 and 5 for explorations of these pedagogies.) All are cross-listed from other departments (Theology, Education, Political Science), where the instructors are located.

2. JPS 365 *Faith and Moral Development*. Typically, the three one-credit sections that constitute this course are taken over the two semesters of the junior year and the first semester of the senior year, but accommodations can be made as course schedules demand. Recently, a course modeled on Faith and Moral Development has been established as a dedicated academic component of the Cortina Community, a sophomore residential program named for Fr. Jon Cortina, a Jesuit engineer, professor, and rural pastor who would have been murdered along with his six brother Jesuits of the University of Central America had he not been elsewhere that fateful night in San Salvador. JPS 265 *Cortina Seminar* takes its themes from the four Pillars (values) of the Cortina Community: *community*, *service*, *faith*, and *justice*. JPS 265 may be substituted for one semester of JPS 365 for students who elect to pursue the JPS minor. (See Chapter 6 for an exploration of the pedagogy of studying moral exemplars.)

3. *A course teaching skills of social analysis* in either Sociology or Political Science. The following course titles indicate the subjects covered within the menu of options: *Social Problems: Values, Issues and Public Policy*; *American Cultural Minorities*; *Social Change*; *Social Inequality and Stratification*; *Politics of the Developing Areas*; *Public Policy and Poverty in the United States*; *Global Poverty and Development*; *Poverty, Development, and Public Policy*. JPS 361, mentioned earlier, is a six-credit course that includes substantial social analysis of the Dominican Republic (DR) reality, and also meets this requirement.

4. JPS 565 *Catholic Social Teaching*. Cross-listed with Theology, this course critically examines the major documents of Catholic social ethics, the teaching of the Popes and bishops from *Rerum Novarum* (*Of New Things*) in 1891 to the present. As a service-learning or an immersion course is the experiential heart of the program, so is this course its normative core. Every Catholic college and university ought to have such a course, but obviously I do not believe that any single course, no matter how well taught, can fully advance the cause of Catholic social *learning*.[18]

5. JPS 588 *Christian Ethics of War and Peace*. Also cross-listed with Theology, this course examines Christian ethical perspectives on the use of lethal force from biblical times to the present day. Just war,

pacifism, and nonviolence are considered from both Catholic and Protestant perspectives. The relationships between justice and peace, needless to say, are fraught; that really is the crux of the pedagogical dialectic of the syllabus, in the manner of Abelard's *Sic et Non*.[19] Beginning in 2009, considerably more attention has been given to the application of ethical perspectives to wars of the United States. This case study approach emphasizes the development of practical reasoning or reflective judgment[20] and also awareness of one's social location: that is, critical contexualization of an otherwise abstract theological debate.

6. *JPS 499 Senior Seminar*. This course is the capstone for the program and poses two questions: How is social justice actually pursued, and how does one discern a vocation within the wide range of professional options? The first question is addressed through visits to an inner-city school, a community health center, a shelter for the homeless, and a legal clinic serving low-income clients. Guest speakers in the classroom also address professional social work, the social contributions of business, community organizing, church programs of service and immersion, public office, and philanthropy.[21] Vocational discernment is addressed in part through the reading of *The Book of Mev*, Mark Chmiel's remarkable memoir of his late wife Mev Puleo and her own struggles and insights in discovering her calling. This narrative is complemented by the study and personal appropriation of Dean Brackley's *The Call to Discernment in Troubled Times: New Perspectives on the Transformative Wisdom of Ignatius of Loyola*, and by a closing conversation with a well-known Jesuit spiritual director.[22] The students prepare a portfolio of their writings and other materials as testimony to the state of their own vocational discernment as they prepare to graduate from college and enter the gritty reality of the world.

The Justice and Peace Studies minor can be combined with almost any major,[23] which emphasizes that social concern is not limited to full-time activists but can be an integral dimension of any profession. The Justice and Society major, on the other hand, co-sponsored by the Justice and Peace Studies Program and the Sociology and Anthropology Department, was designed for students preparing for careers in social change. It combines the six courses of the JPS minor with the minor in Sociology, which includes an introductory course, *Research Methods in the Social Sciences*, *Statistics for the Social Sciences*, and *Social and Cultural Theory*. The 37-credit major also included three electives: two from Sociology or Anthropology and one of thematic relevance to the major from another department.

Because simply listing and describing these courses may not tell the whole story, Figure 8.1 shows how the courses are placed on the Pedagogical Circle as presented in Chapter 2. This diagram might serve as a template for the design or redesign of programs at other schools.

Curricular and Paracurricular Contexts

Of course, these six courses do not exist in isolation from the rest of the undergraduate curriculum and each student's major. The Creighton University College of Arts & Sciences Core Curriculum, in addition to required courses in composition, literature, foreign language, art or communication, history (both Western and non-Western) natural science, and mathematics, also requires courses that at least indirectly support the themes of the Pedagogical Circle: two courses in the human sciences, three in theology, two in philosophy,

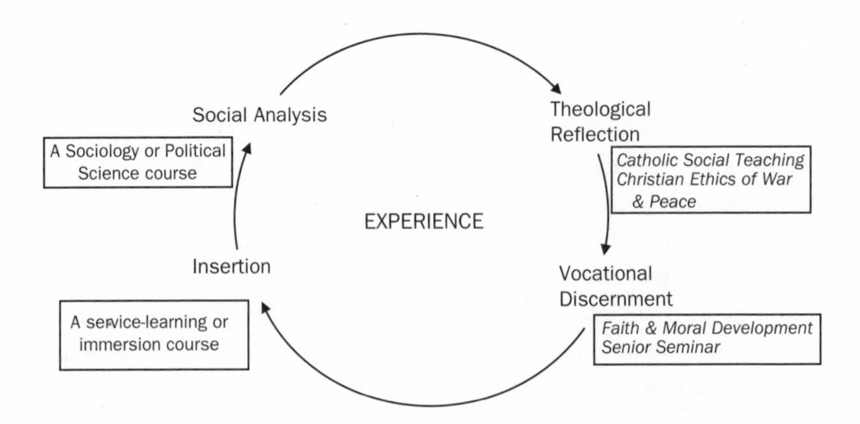

Figure 8.1. The Justice and Peace Studies Minor on the Pedagogical Circle

one in ethics, one in global studies, and one on a contemporary ethical concern taught from an interdisciplinary perspective. Majors in any of the social sciences and theology obviously complement the objectives of the JPS minor, but students have also found ways to integrate the minor with, for example, a chemistry or English major.

Nor does the curriculum as a whole exist in isolation from the rest of the students' lives in organizations, clubs, and residence halls, many of which promote leadership and service. In particular, the Creighton Center for Service and Justice (CCSJ) has led the way in creating a culture of community engagement on campus. Many of the students in the Justice and Peace Studies Program are active through the CCSJ in weekly service opportunities in Omaha, fall and spring break service trips throughout the country, the annual Ignatian Family Teach-In, summer internships, and other related events and programs. To suggest just some of the symbiosis at play here, a Justice and Society graduate is now the Assistant Director of the CCSJ and offers a section of Faith and Moral Development especially designed for the core team of CCSJ student leaders. Finally, to give one last example of campus culture, the Institute for Latin American Concern (now directed by another Justice and Society graduate) has offered summer health clinics in remote areas of the Dominican Republic for three decades. The clinics are staffed by Creighton health professionals and students but also by undergraduate *ayudantes* (helpers), all of whom live with Dominican families of low income and limited opportunity. This provides yet another powerful insertion or immersion experience for a small number of students each year.

The Justice and Peace Studies Program has been effective in no small part because it has been so well supported by these surrounding curricular and para-curricular opportunities. I am deeply grateful to all my colleagues who make them possible.

Listening to Student Voices

That is the story of Catholic social learning at one university. But how is that story told by the students themselves? Because so many of my students have studied in either the Dominican Republic or El Salvador (or both), and because those have been profoundly formative experiences for them and thereby produce their most compelling writing, almost all of these anonymous selections speak of those experiences and what they have meant to the students.[24] I assemble them (very lightly edited) not to make any new argument, but to illustrate some of the arguments already made in the previous pages. *And to humble and inspire the adult readers of this book.*

Confused and Feeling Ashamed

As a freshman, even before participating in *Encuentro Dominicano* as a sophomore, this student was beginning to ask the big questions: "I have found a new interest in figuring out what I am called to do with my life and how I can use my education for that." In response to a new awareness of the meaning of compassion ("'to suffer with'") and its centrality to Christian faith, as proposed in her introductory theology course, she found herself "*confused and feeling ashamed* of thinking of actually pursuing becoming a doctor, when I should just pack up and leave for a third-world country and be a servant to them" (emphasis added). But she also comes to realize that her newfound sense of Christian vocation "could mean pursuing a medical degree but not necessarily using the degree for personal benefits such as a nice car or house, but to help other people in different communities who lack medical technologies."

God as an Alarm Clock

A graduate of a Catholic high school had already traveled to a Third World country before starting college. In a paper written for Faith and Moral Development, he reported that through this experience he "was awakened physically and spiritually to the injustices of the world. . . . It was like an enormous alarm clock for my life going off but I didn't want to get up. I didn't want to be burdened with these problems. I wanted to go back to dreamland and pretend nothing happened, but

I knew I couldn't bury it. The feeling was so real, so God-like that after while I felt blessed to have received it."

Ineffable and Noetic

Inspired by the language of a text we were reading for class, a student reflected on the "ineffable" and "noetic" quality of his experiences in the DR. In particular he found those qualities in his relationships with poor Dominicans: "Coming from a society that values material goods and holds one's social status in high regard, it was very humbling, and defied the reasoning I inherited from my own culture, to learn and grow from the example and wisdom of the *campesinos*."

The Poorest, Weakest Person

A student was inspired by Gandhi's "talisman," discovered while studying the Mahatma in a section of Faith and Moral Development. Gandhi advocates making decisions in times of doubt or self-absorption so as to benefit the poorest and weakest person you have ever encountered.[25] The student reported that "the weakest, poorest person I have ever seen was a young boy, not more than 10 years old, on the International Highway between the DR and Haiti. He sat outside his hut and waited for trucks to pass on the road. The traffic was sparse, but when a truck came bouncing over the treacherous road (his front yard), he would start running alongside the truck begging for change in a language I could not understand. This young boy was naked, with a belly bloated by hunger, and had large tumors on his stomach and back. . . . He is out there today begging for handouts from passing trucks. Is there any vocation potential for him? I think about him every day. I do not know his name, but I saw his face and his pain and there was nothing I could do about it. How can my actions, now as a student in Omaha, empower this young boy? This is Gandhi's talisman, and it keeps me grounded whenever I am faced with decisions that impact the lives of others."

A Sad Vision, a New Passion

Another student had a similar experience in El Salvador. "The grandmother of my Salvadoran family once told me through the three or four teeth she had left in her mouth: 'It's not easy being poor. It is such a hard life. The difficulties never cease.' Her sad eyes and wrinkles told the story of her suffering every day, but for the first time, she expressed the pain of poverty to me in words. She then resumed her fit of coughing due to the lung problems she had accrued from a life of cooking over an open fire and receiving inadequate health care. In the background, I caught a glimpse of the nine-year-old I had come to know as my *hermana*, or sister, making tortillas crouched over the smoking fire. I saw a sad vision of what Ana's future would hold if she lived the same life as her grandmother. At that moment I knew the trajectory of my life had to change. I decided I must live my life in a way that honors my Salvadoran family and the struggle of so many people in similar circumstances. When I left the little town of Guarjila, El Salvador, I did not know *how* I would to it, but I knew that working to improve the lives of impoverished people would be my life's work. A passion for social justice entered my world."

What Is the Point of This?

Despite the commonality of themes in these encounters, each student processes her experience in her own unique and life-giving way. The following was written as a Daily Reflection for Creighton's internationally known Collaborative Ministry Web site. "I'm studying in the Dominican Republic this semester. I spend time each week at a nursing home called Hospicio for people who have nowhere else to live and can no longer live on their own. Every morning, the women who live there organize themselves and pray the Rosary in the chapel. The woman I generally visit, Sarita, doesn't like to go into the chapel to pray, but she says the prayers from the hallway while we sit together. While she prays, I'm left with time to think—I sometimes say the prayers with her but I'm at a point where I feel very insincere doing so, so I generally choose to sit quietly. Most of the time, my thoughts wander to the question, 'What is the point of this?' Why are these people, most of them abandoned by their families, here? Why do they suffer? What is it that they're praying for? And how is it that they keep praying in the face of it all?

"I read a lot about how being a Christian demands that I be counter-cultural. I'm learning that being 'counter-cultural' is a lot more complicated than I ever imagined it to be. It means seeing the old woman, whose Spanish I do not have a prayer of understanding, as completely my equal in God's eyes—and more importantly, acting in a way that realizes that equality. It means doing the same with my classmates. But it also means understanding that prayer isn't just another manner of purchasing an item from God.com with the option for express, overnight delivery. The women at Hospicio pray. They just pray. Of course, I don't know all of their thoughts and maybe the truth is that they are fed up with it sometimes. However, I do know that they pray every morning. And when they come out of the chapel, they greet me with smiles and embraces and not a trace of weariness—women who, in my mind, have every reason to be irritated and weary. I'm reminded of how my values—the world's standards—can be so horribly off."

Washing Feet

For this student, it didn't take a magnificent church, beautiful music, or an inspiring homily to experience the Gospel message during Holy Week. During her semester in the Dominican Republic, she volunteered at Caritas, an international organization that feeds children one meal a day during the school week. "I don't know if Jesus had four rich college kids, a bar of Irish Spring soap, the bathroom sponge, the mopping bucket, and a borrowed towel in mind when he ordered his disciples to wash the feet of others, but nonetheless, we thought this was a pretty decent interpretation of the gospel. We picked twelve of our beloved Caritas kids, read the Holy Thursday Gospel to them, and each one of us washed three pairs of tiny feet. Feet cracked and broken from gravel roads and no shoes. Feet with scabs and open wounds from lack of medical access. Feet covered in dirt and other unclean substances. Feet of third world children who do not have enough to eat. And so we washed their feet. We soaped up the sponge and scrubbed as hard as we could. I know I was trying to scrub away my sin that manifests itself in the broken feet of innocent children. I was trying to apologize for wearing my sixty dollar sandals when they rarely had shoes that fit. I was trying to help them which is something I realized I may never be able to do. The only thing I could do was love them. And as little children always do, they eagerly loved me right back."

Geography and Faith

Especially in El Salvador, the tension students experience because of their new awareness can be "almost unbearable," as another student put it. On the one hand, she met or learned of many moral exemplars: "[I]t was through the stories of such figures as Oscar Romero, Jean Donovan, Jon Cortina, Ignacio Ellacuría, Dean Brackley, Ita Ford, Rutilio Grande, and many, many more that I began to understand and *feel* my faith for the first time in a very long time. . . . It was in El Salvador that I began to understand the Gospel message of Jesus and the way in which one's faith can really serve the oppressed people of the world. . . . The more I learned about the religious movement in El Salvador [before, during, and after the civil war of the 1980s], the more I fell in love with my faith and the power of Liberation Theology. Yet, the more I learned about the war in El Salvador, the suffering of the people, and the intentionality of it all, the more disgusted I became with my connection to the oppressor. . . . It is a fact; I am connected to both the injustice and justice, the oppressor and the oppressed, the crucifixion and the resurrection."

Reflecting on that tension for a writing assignment helped her "to understand my place in a world where by geography I have been born into kinship with a government I find at times very unjust, but where by faith I have been born into kinship with the People of God."

And that, dear reader, is proximate to where this book began for me many years ago, on the U.S. border with the Two-Thirds World.

Today, thanks in particular to my students, I feel less alone straddling that divide and a good deal more hopeful. The Spirit lives.

Eleven Theses on Student Vocational Development in the Catholic University

The following theses may be helpful in thematizing these student reflections and summarizing the major ideas of this book.

1. To be called or to have a vocation is to have one's imagination captured by an experience, story, vision, or symbol larger than oneself.
2. Young adults are particularly ripe for the experience of vocation because they have begun to think of themselves as responsible for their own moral and spiritual lives, and because what they will be when they grow up is no longer a fantasy question.
3. Young adults are capable of a more mature self-consciousness than they were as adolescents, and so are better able to enter into healthy, probing reflection on fundamental issues such as identity, vocation, faith, and commitment.
4. Just as young adults are capable of a probing self-reflection, so are they capable of a critical engagement with their world. Community service, service-learning courses, and cross-cultural immersion experiences are indispensable opportunities where self and world enter into new relationships.
5. Narratives and exemplars of faithful, reflective commitment to an authentic self and a more just and peaceful world can mentor young adults in their own quests for similar commitments.
6. Young adults need communities of peers who share commitment to the quest.
7. Faith traditions, mediated by sympathetic mentors, can provide a larger framework of meaning and wisdom to nourish and guide young adults' development of integrity and purpose.
8. The dominant culture of the United States is, at least, a distraction: at worst, an enemy to the young adult quest for a sense of

vocation. Careerism, the cult of sex and personality, conspicuous consumption, the mirage of power and control, the numbness of media glut, the pressure to conform, and the denial of death all conspire to deprive young adults of the challenges of wrestling with "big questions" and shaping "worthy dreams."[26]

9. Universities have enormous opportunities and responsibilities to foster young adult vocational development, and Catholic universities have privileged resources with which to meet these opportunities and responsibilities, but they, too, are challenged by their cultural context.
10. To the extent that such universities bring their resources into critical dialogue with the dominant culture and contemporary world, a world of massive suffering and injustice, they provide a mentoring model and context for their young adult students. To the extent they do not, they have no *Catholic* reason to exist.
11. The distinctive educational mission of the Catholic university is recapitulated in the preceding theses 1–10.

NOTES

Preface

1. See Daniel K. Lapsley and Darcia Narvaez, eds., *Moral Development, Self, and Identity* (Mahwah, N.J.:Lawrence Erlbaum, 2004), which includes my "Identity as Motivation: Toward a Theory of the Moral Self," 21–46.

2. A standard collection is David J. O'Brien & Thomas A. Shannon, eds. *Catholic Social Thought: The Documentary Heritage* (Maryknoll, N.Y.: Orbis, 1992).

3. "Faithjustice" is shorthand for "the faith that does justice" and social Catholicism generally. See, for example, the excellent book by Fred Kammer, S.J., with its *double entendre* title, *Doing Faithjustice: An Introduction to Catholic Social Thought*, 2nd Ed. (New York: Paulist Press, 2004).

1. Personal Encounter: The Only Way

1. Carolyn Forché, *The Country Between Us* (New York: Harper & Row, 1981), 16. Used with the gracious permission of the author.

2. The Atlacatl Battalion, which was responsible for the murders of the six Jesuits and two women at the University of Central America in San Salvador on November 16, 1989, was "an elite group organized by U.S. trainers in the early 1980s as a crack

counter-terrorism force, and has been frequently implicated in human rights abuses. The most famous was the massacre of over seven hundred civilians in the town of Morazón in 1981, immediately following the battlion's initial training at Fr. Benning, Georgia. A professor at the army training school once joked that 'we've had a hard time getting [them] to take prisoners instead of ears.'" Stan Granot Duncan, from his "Introduction: The Crime," in Jon Sobrino, Ignacio Ellacuría, and Others, *Companions of Jesus: The Jesuit Martyrs of El Salvador* (Maryknoll, N.Y.: Orbis Books, 1990), xv. As I heard Forché read "The Colonel" in March of 1980, apparently the collecting of ears preceded (but continued with) the formation of the Atlacatl Battalion.

3. See the biography by James R. Brockman, *Romero: A Life: The Essential Biography of a Modern Martyr and Christian Hero* (Maryknoll, N.Y.: Orbis Books, 2005). Also see Dean Brackley, S.J., *The University and Its Martyrs: Hope from Central America*, 3rd ed. (San Salvador: Centro Monseñor Romero, Universidad Centroamericano "Jose Simeón Cañas," 2008) for an extensive bibliography on El Salvador and Central America.

4. For an overview of this sea change in Latin American Catholicism, see Curt Cadorette, M.M., "Medellin" and "Puebla," in *The New Dictionary of Catholic Social Thought*, ed. Judith A. Dwyer (Collegeville, Minn.; Michael Glazier, 1994), 590–94 and 797–801, respectively.

5. The writings of and about liberation theology are vast. For a brief overview, see the entry by Gustavo Gutiérrez in *The New Dictionary of Catholic Social Thought*, 548–53. See the following footnote.

6. Gutiérrez is often called the "father" of liberation theology because of his seminal book, *A Theology of Liberation* (Maryknoll, N.Y.: Orbis Books, 1988; originally published in Spanish in 1971 and in English in 1973).

7. Jon Sobrino, S.J., *Christology at the Crossroads* (Maryknoll, N.Y.: Orbis Books, 1978). Sobrino is the premier liberation Christologian; see his more recent books, *Jesus the Liberator: A Historical-Theological Reading of Jesus of Nazareth* and *Christ the Liberator: A View from the Victims* (Maryknoll, N.Y.: Orbis Books, 1993 and 2001, respectively).

8. Juan Luis Segundo, S.J., *The Liberation of Theology* (Maryknoll, N.Y.: Orbis Books, 1976).

9. Penny Lernoux, *Cry of the People: United States Involvement in the Rise of Fascism, Torture, and Murder and the Persecution of the Catholic Church in Latin America* (New York: Doubleday, 1980).

10. The standard collection of documents by the popes and bishops on "the social question" is David J. O'Brien and Thomas A. Shannon, ed., *Catholic Social Thought: The Documentary Heritage* (Maryknoll, N.Y.: 1992). All citations of CST documents will be to the texts as found in this volume and will use abbreviations of the titles and paragraph number (or page number when paragraphs are not numbered, as in JW). The texts are also available online at various locations. A Web site tied to what its editor, Kenneth R. Himes, O.F.M., justly calls "the standard reference work for the major documents of Catholic social teaching," *Modern Catholic Social Teaching: Commentaries and Interpretations*

(Washington, D.C.: Georgetown, 2005), can be found at http://www2.bc.edu/~khimes/publications/mcst.

11. For a brief overview, see Sr. Patricia Jacobsen, M.M., "God Came to El Salvador," in *Witnesses of Hope: The Persecution of Christians in Latin America*, ed. Martin Lange and Reinhold Iblacker, S.J. (Maryknoll, N.Y.: Orbis Books, 1981), 141–53. See also the video documentary by Ana Carrigan, *Roses in December: The Story of Jean Donovan* (New York: First-Run Features, 1982).

12. *Studia Mystica*, Vol. V, No. 4 (Winter 1982), 48.

13. For her life story, see the in-every-way-remarkable book by her husband Mark Chmiel, *The Book of Mev* (Bloomington, Ind.: Xlibris, 2005). For a brief but eloquent overview of her life, see Robert Ellsberg, *All Saints* (New York: Crossroad, 1997), 25–27.

14. Mev Puleo, *The Struggle Is One: Visions and Voices of Liberation* (Albany: SUNY Press, 1994).

15. Puleo, *The Struggle Is One*, 1.

16. I am sympathetic to John Haughey's belief "that Christians will stand pat in their attitude toward justice and the injustices that surround them until they see the ideal the Church is preaching incarnated in the person of Jesus." See his essay, "Jesus as the Justice of God," in *The Faith That Does Justice: Examining the Christian Sources for Social Change*, ed. John C. Haughey, S.J. (New York: Paulist Press, 1977), 264–90; see 264.

17. The first volume of the *Journal of Catholic Social Thought*, published at Villanova University, appeared in Winter, 2004.

18. See John F. Kavanaugh, S.J., and Mev Puleo, *Faces of Poverty, Faces of Christ* (Maryknoll, N.Y.: Orbis Books, 1991).

19. Both Tijuana poems appeared in *Sojourners*,Vol. 11, No. 5 (May 1982), 17.

20. Daniel Maguire, "The Feminist Turn in Social Ethics," *Mainstreaming Feminist Research for Teaching Religious Studies*, ed. Arlene Swidler and Walter E. Conn (Lanham, Md.: University Press of America, 1985), 77–83; see 78 (emphasis added).

21. Most of the Church's social teaching appears in the form of papal encyclical letters. "Encyclical" simply means formally but openly circulated. Leo XIII addressed the first modern social encyclical, *Rerum Novarum* (1891) to the bishops of the church. John XXIII addressed *Pacem in Terris* (1963) to "all men of good will" and John Paul II *Sollicitudo Rei Socialis* (1987) to "all people of good will." This marks a certain "democratization" in the magisterium's sense of who is responsible for enacting their words.

22. John R. Popiden, "Paul VI," in Judith A. Dwyer, ed., *The New Dictionary of Catholic Social Thought* (Collegeville, Minn.: The Liturgical Press, 1994), 714.

23. I have lost the source in which the three principles were enurmerated. Fr. Curran, who graciously took up my query, could not locate it himself. He did affirm these three foundational principles of Catholic social teaching: the human person as possessing an innate dignity because created in the image of God, the social or communal nature of the human person, and the goods of the earth as created for the benefit of all.

24. Kenneth R. Himes, O.F.M., *Responses to 101 Questions on Catholic Social Teaching* (Mahwah, N.J.: Paulist Press, 2001).

25. E.g., *Forming Consciences for Faithful Citizenship: A Call to Political Responsibility from the Catholic Bishops of the United States* (Washington, D.C.: United States Conference of Catholic Bishops, 2007).

26. May be found online at http://www.usccb.org/sdwp/international/ACatholic FrameworkforEconomicLife.pdf.

27. William J. Byron, "Ten Building Blocks of Catholic Social Teaching," *America*, Oct. 31, 1998.

28. *Brothers and Sisters to Us*, the U.S. Bishops' Pastoral Letter on Racism in Our Day (National Conference of Catholic Bishops, 1979), at only 14 pages, is hardly a major document and is not included in O'Brien and Shannon. The seven-page index of that collection does not even include an entry on race or racism (although a few mentions can be found in the texts themselves); the citations for discrimination are not only scanty but woefully underdeveloped. *The New Dictionary of Catholic Social Thought* includes no entry for race or racism although it does treat related issues. The most developed (40 pages in booklet form) statement, *The Church and Racism: Towards a More Fraternal Society* (St. Paul Books and Media, no date), produced by the Pontifical Commission Justice and Peace in 1988, is virtually unknown and is not available from the Publications Office of the U.S. Conference of Catholic Bishops. Marvin L. Mich, in his excellent historical analysis, *Catholic Social Teaching and Movements* (Mystic, Conn.: Twenty-Third Publications, 1998), although it includes a chapter on the church and racism (largely lamenting the lack of connection), ironically does not mention it.

29. Thomas Massaro, S.J., *Living Justice: Catholic Social Teaching in Action* (Franklin, Wisc.: Sheed & Ward, 2000).

30. See Chapter 2 of Paulo Freire, *Pedadogy of the Oppressed* (New York: Continuum, 1994).

31. The Pontifical Commission Justice and Peace, established by Paul VI in 1967 as mandated by the Second Vatican Council's *Gaudium et Spes* (1965), published a series of booklets commenting on *Justice in the World*. The booklet on "Education and Justice" (1973) by S. Mary Linscott, S.N.D., "does not attempt to explore questions of technique or methodology, nor in any other way undertake the kind of analysis customary among professional educators" (p. 10). The current book attempts to do just that.

32. I reproduce the patriarchal language of CST as is, but with apologies to all readers.

33. Freire's first book, *Educação como prãtica da liberade (Education as the Practice of Freedom)*, was published in Brazil in 1967, according to Richard Schaull in his introduction to *Pedagogy of the Oppressed* (New York: Continuum, 1970, 13), which itself was published in English in the year before the *Justice in the World* Synod, which met in the fall of 1971.

34. See Freire, *Pedagogy*, 17, and Chapter 3 for a definition and full explication of this pedagogical process.

35. Dan Hartnett, S.J., "The Heuristics of Justice," *Proceedings of the 65th Annual Meeting of the Jesuit Philosophical Association* (2004), 61. See also Monika K. Hellwig, "Good News to the Poor: Do They Understand It Better?" in *Tracing the Spirit: Communities, Social Action, and Theological Reflection*," ed. James E. Hug, S.J. (Ramsey, N.J.: Paulist Press, 1983), 122–48.

36. Recommended titles include Monika Hellwig, *The Eucharist and the Hunger of the World* (Lanham, Md.: Sheed & Ward, 1992); Mark Searle, ed., *Liturgy and Social Justice* (Collegeville, Minn.; The Liturgical Press, 1980); E. Byron Anderson and Bruce T. Morrill, eds., *Liturgy and the Moral Self: Humanity at Full Stretch Before God—Essays in Honor of Don E. Saliers* (Collegeville, Minn.; The Liturgical Press, 1998); Megan McKenna, *Rites of Justice: The Sacraments and Liturgy as Ethical Imperatives* (Maryknoll, N.Y.: Orbis Books, 1997); Kathleen Hughes and Mark Francis, eds., *Living No Longer for Ourselves: Liturgy and Justice in the Nineties* (Collegeville, Minn.: The Liturgical Press, 1991). Thanks to Fr. Roc O'Connor, S.J., for these recommendations.

2. Ignatian Pedagogy and the Faith That Does Justice

1. John W. O'Malley, S.J., "How the First Jesuits Became Involved in Education," in *The Jesuit* Ratio Studiorum: *400th Anniversary Perspectives*, ed. Vincent J. Duminuco, S.J. (New York: Fordham University Press, 2000), 57.

2. Duminuco, *The Jesuit* Ratio Studiorum, x (citing Gilbert Highet, a well-known teacher and scholar of classics at Columbia University from 1938 to 1971). All subsequent page citations in this chapter are to this volume.

3. *Sollicitudo Omnium Ecclesiaarum*, quoted in "Characteristics," in Duminuco, 229.

4. I have heard it said that there are only three recognizable "brands" in higher education: "Oxbridge," Ivy, and Jesuit.

5. This is not to make an exclusive claim for Jesuit education or Ignatian pedagogy, as I hope the rest of the chapter and book demonstrates.

6. For an overview of beginnings of this ongoing national project by one of the early and influential organizers, see William C. Spohn, "The University That Does Justice," *Conversations*, Spring, 2001, 4–12.

7. Available online at http://www.creighton.edu/fileadmin/user/CCAS/departments/SocAnt/docs/Education_for_Justice_Self-Study.pdf.

8. More historically distant antecedents will be discussed in Chapter 7.

9. E.g., Ronald Modras, "Pedro Arrupe," *Ignatian Humanism* (Chicago: Loyola Press, 2004), 283.

10. Peter-Hans Kolvenbach, S.J., "Foreword," in *Pedro Arrupe: Essential Writings*, ed. Kevin Burke, S.J. (Maryknoll, N.Y.: Orbis Books, 2004): 12.

11. Burke, *Pedro Arrupe*, 22.

12. Modras, "Pedro Arrupe," 246–47.

13. Burke, *Pedro Arrupe*, 22.

14. Pedro Arrupe, S.J., "Conscientization and Solidarity," in Burke, 86–87.

15. Ibid., 87–88.

16. Burke, *Pedro Arrupe*, 173.

17. Arrupe, "Conscientization," in Burke, 176.

18. Ibid., 187.

19. Thomas Clarke, S.J., in a classic essay, "Option for the Poor: A Reflection," parses the meaning of the option "through several propositions and a conjunction: [1] the non-poor "are all called to act *for* or on behalf of the poor, . . . [2] the poor have the Good News preached *to* them. . . . [3] the most effective bearers of the Good News to the poor will be those who . . . walk *with* the poor, . . . [4] some . . . will receive the gift of living and working . . . *as* poor. . . . [5] the culminating point . . . the Gospel . . . goes forth . . . *from the poor*" (*America*, January 30, 1988, 99; italics in original). The last three relationships—*with*, *as*, and *from*—caution against any taint of *noblesse oblige* or elitist patronage in the first two—*for* and *to*. Perhaps the full ideal of Jesuit education (the "magis") would be to pursue all five.

20. I cannot help remarking that a similar pedagogy, in the dissimilar context of public education, is articulated by John Dewey in *Experience and Education* (New York: Simon and Schuster, 1938/1997).

21. Available online at http://www.creighton.edu/CollaborativeMinistry/kolvenbach_speech.html.

22. For the history, metaphysics, ethics, and theology of solidarity in CST, see the entry by Matthew Lamb in *The New Dictionary of Catholic Social Thought*, ed. Judith A. Dwyer (Collegeville, Minn.: Michael Glazier, 1994), 908–12.

23. John Paul II, *Sollicitudo Rei Socialis*, #38, 40; in O'Brien and Shannon, *Catholic Social Thought* (Maryknoll, N.Y.: Orbis Books, 1992), 421–23 (emphasis in original).

24. Mark Chmiel, *The Book of Mev* (Bloomington, Ind.: Xlibris, 2005), 54.

25. Fr. Kolvenbach, in the same address, adds the example of the academic researcher: "By preference, by option, our Jesuit point of view is that of the poor. So our professors' commitment to faith and justice entails a most significant shift in viewpoint and choice of values. Adopting the point of view of those who suffer injustice, our professors seek the truth and share their search and its results with our students. . . . To expect our professors to make such an explicit option and speak about it is obviously not easy; it entails risks. But I do believe that this is what Jesuit educators have publicly stated, in Church and in society, to be our defining commitment."

26. Dean Brackley, S.J., *The Call to Discernment in Troubled Times: New Perspectives on the Transformative Wisdom of Ignatius of Loyola* (New York: Crossroad, 2004), 57–58.

27. Joe Holland and Peter Henriot, S.J., *Social Analysis: Linking Faith and Justice* (Maryknoll, N.Y.: Orbis Books, 1983).

28. Frans Wijsen, Peter Henriot, and Rodrigo Mejia, eds., *The Pastoral Circle Revisited: A Critical Quest for Truth and Transformation* (Maryknoll, N.Y.: Orbis Books, 2005), xxi.

29. Juan Luis Segundo, *The Liberation of Theology* (Maryknoll, N.Y.: Orbis Books), Chapter 1.

30. Paulo Freire, *Pedagogy of the Oppressed* (New York: Continuum, 1994), 33.

31. Ibid., 51.

32. Ibid., 51.

33. Ibid., 48.

34. Ibid., 109.

35. Thomas Massaro, S.J., "From Industrialization to Globalization," in *Living the Catholic Social Tradition: Cases and Commentary*, ed. Kathleen Maas Weigert and Alexia K. Kelley (Lanham, Md.: Rowman & Littlefield, 2005), 45.

36. Marvin L. Mich, *Catholic Social Teaching and Movements* (Mystic, Conn.: Twenty-Third Publications, 1998), 74.

37. Mich, 86; emphasis in original. The archives of the Christian Family Movement and the Young Christian Students are housed at the University of Notre Dame and are available online at http://archives.nd.edu/findaids/ead/html/CFM.htm and at http://archives.nd.edu/findaids/ead/html/YCS.htm.

38. Joe Holland, "Introduction: Roots of the Pastoral Circle in Personal Experiences and Catholic Social Tradition," in *The Pastoral Circle Revisited*, 9.

39. Ibid., 9.

40. Ibid., 10.

41. Ibid., 11.

42. Ibid., 9.

43. See Chapter 7 on the Catholic University.

44. In service, service-learning, and immersion contexts, personal reflection is crucial for student development. To make such reflection at least implicitly Ignatian and yet very accessible, I have often used and recommended these simple reflection guidelines from Dean Brackley, which he developed as a service-learning teacher at Fordham University: "I found that my students greatly benefited from a simple exercise: writing a one-page reflection sheet telling, on the one hand, what they found particularly nourishing or life-giving in the community service that week and, on the other hand, what they found disturbing or confusing. What was it that especially touched their hearts? (I was looking for what Ignatius of Loyola calls 'consolation' and 'desolation.') Then they were to explain briefly why they were so affected." Dean Brackley, S.J., "The Christian University and Liberation: The Challenge of the UCA," *Discovery: Jesuit International Ministries* 2 (December 1992), 13.

3. Teaching Justice After MacIntyre: Toward a Catholic Philosophy of Moral Education

A version of this chapter was published in *Catholic Education: A Journal of Inquiry and Practice* 12/1 (September 2008): 7–24. I wish to express my gratitude to the editors for permission to use it here, and to the editors and anonymous reviewers for comments that led to substantial improvements in the original submission.

1. Aristotle, *The Nicomachean Ethics*, trans. David W. Ross (Oxford, U.K.: Oxford University Press, 1988).

2. Lawrence Kohlberg, *Essays on Moral Development: Volume I: The Philosophy of Moral Development* (San Francisco: Harper & Row, 1981).

3. Lawrence Kohlberg, *Essays on Moral Development: Volume II: The Psychology of Moral Development* (San Francisco: Harper & Row, 1984).

4. Quoted in Maguire, "The Feminist Turn," 78.

5. Lawrence Kohlberg, "Education for Justice: A Modern Statement of the Platonic View," in *Moral Education: Five Lectures*, ed. Nancy F. and Theodore R. Sizer (Cambridge, Mass.: Harvard University Press, 1970), 59.

6. Clark Power, Ann Higgins, and Lawrence Kohlberg, "The Habit of the Common Life: Building Character Through Democratic Community Schools," in *Moral Development and Character Education: A Dialogue*, ed. Larry Nucci (Berkeley: McCutchan, 1989).

7. Alasdair MacIntyre, "Plain Persons and Moral Philosophers: Rules, Virtues, and Goods," in *The MacIntyre Reader*, ed. Kelvin Knight (Notre Dame, Ind.: University of Notre Dame Press, 1998), 136–52. All page references in this section are to this article.

8. Alasdair MacIntyre, *After Virtue: A Study in Moral Theory*, Second Edition (Notre Dame, Ind.: University of Notre Dame Press, 1984); *Whose Justice? Which Rationality?* (Notre Dame, Ind.: University of Notre Dame Press, 1988); *Three Rival Versions of Moral Inquiry: Encyclopedia, Genealogy, and Tradition*: Gifford Lectures, University of Edinburgh, 1988 (Notre Dame, Ind.: University of Notre Dame Press, 1990).

9. Kelvin Knight, "Revolutionary Aristotelianism," in *Contemporary Political Studies* 2 (1996): 885–96.

10. "For an accurate and perceptive discussion of my political views, see Kelvin Knight, 'Revolutionary Aristotelianism.'" MacIntyre, "Politics, Philosophy, and the Common Good," in Knight, *The MacIntyre Reader*, 235.

11. All page citations in this section, unless otherwise noted, are to MacIntyre, "Plain Persons and Moral Philosophers."

12. MacIntyre, *After Virtue*, 187.

13. Aristotle, *The Nicomachean Ethics*, trans. David Ross (Oxford: Oxford University Press, 1998), 1106b36, 39.

14. John J. Horton and Susan Mendus, eds., *After MacIntyre: Critical Perspectives on the Work of Alasdair MacIntyre* (Notre Dame, Ind.: University of Notre Dame Press, 1994), 8.

15. All page citations in this section, unless otherwise noted, are to MacIntyre, *After Virtue*, 216; emphasis in original.

16. See MacIntyre, *Three Rival Versions of Moral Inquiry*.

17. Michael Fuller, *Making Sense of MacIntyre* (Aldershot, U.K.: Ashgate, 1998), 118–19.

18. MacIntyre, "Plain Persons," 146.

19. All page citations in this section, unless otherwise noted, are to Kelvin Knight, "Revolutionary Aristotelianism," 888.

20. Alasdair MacIntyre, *Marxism and Christianity*, Second edition (London: Duckworth, 1995), vii (emphasis added).

21. MacIntyre, *Marxism*, xiv.

22. Ibid., xxxi.

23. Alasdair MacIntyre, "Aquinas's Critique of Education: Against His Own Age, Against Ours," in *Philosophers on Education: New Historical Perspectives*, ed. Amélie Oksenberg Rorty (London: Routledge, 1998), 107 (emphasis in original).

24. All subsequent page citations in this section, unless otherwise noted, are to Alasdair MacIntyre, "How to Seem Virtuous without Actually Being So," in *Education in Morality*, ed. J. Mark Halstead and Terence H. McLaughlin (London: Routledge, 1999), 118–31.

25. E.g., William J. Bennett, *The Book of Virtues: A Treasury of Great Moral Stories* (New York: Simon & Schuster, 1993), 11; Thomas Lickona, *Educating for Character: How Our Schools Can Teach Respect and Responsibility* (New York: Bantam, 1991), 50; Madonna M. Murphy, *Character Education in America's Blue Ribbon Schools: Best Practices for Meeting the Challenges*, Second edition (Lanham, Md.: Scarecrow Press, 2002), 10, 13, 191; Kevin Ryan and Karen Bohlin, *Building Character in Schools: Practical Ways to Bring Moral Instruction to Life* (San Francisco: Jossey-Bass, 1999), 19, 48, 181, 195.

26. Aristotle, *The Nicomachean Ethics*, trans. David Ross (Oxford: Oxford University Press, 1998).

27. MacIntyre, "Aquinas's Critique," 107 (emphasis in original).

28. MacIntyre, *After Virtue*, 263.

29. Ibid., 263. For a remarkably parallel analysis of education in ancient Israel, see Walter Brueggemann, "Passion and perspective: two dimensions of education in the bible," in *Theological Perspectives on Christian Formation: A Reader on Theology and Christian Education*, ed. Jeff Astley, Leslie J. Francis, and Colin Crowder (Grand Rapids, Mich.: Eerdmans: 1996), 71–79. "What does it mean to be Israel? . . . The answer is . . . to tell the story of this community. . . . [which] has a distinct identity that is in considerable tension with the values and the presuppositions of the dominant community. That distinct identity is the primary subject matter of education in passion. . . . Such nurture in passion leads to particular practices of passion in the public life of the people" (71–72).

30. Ibid., 69.

31. All subsequent page citations in this section, unless otherwise noted, are to David Hollenbach, "A communitarian reconstruction of human rights: contributions from Catholic tradition," in *Catholicism and Liberalism: Contributions to American Public Philosophy*, ed. R. Bruce Douglass and David Hollenbach (Cambridge, U.K.: Cambridge University Press, 1994), 127–50.

32. *Gaudium et Spes* can be found in O'Brien and Shannon, *Catholic Social Thought*, 166–237; the quotations are from #30 and 24.

33. Ibid., 131–62.

34. Ibid., #79.

4. Immersion, Empathy, and Perspective Transformation: *Semestre Dominicano*, 1998

1. *Semestre Dominicano* has since been restructured and renamed *Encuentro Dominicano* (Dominican Encounter).

2. The United Nations rates countries according to a Human Development Index (HDI), based on three factors—life expectancy, educational attainment, and income—on a scale of 0.0 to 1.0. In 2006, the HDI for the United States was 0.940; for the Dominican Republic, 0.701; and for Haiti, 0.360.

3. For an analysis of U.S. media coverage of Aristide up to November, 1993, see my "Recent U.S. Perceptions of Haiti and Haitians," *Journal for Peace and Justice Studies* 5/2 (1993), 133–44.

4. Russell A. Butkus, "Moral Education, Peace, and Social Justice," in *Education for Peace and Justice*, ed. Padraic O'Hare (San Francisco: Harper & Row, 1983), 155 (emphasis added).

5. William Bean Kennedy, "The Ideological Captivity of the Non-Poor," in *Pedagogies for the Non-Poor*, ed. Alice Frazer Evans, Robert A. Evans, and William Bean Kennedy (Maryknoll, N.Y.: Orbis Books, 1987), 237.

6. For one "state of the art" perspective, see James Rest, Darcia Narvaez, Muriel J. Bebeau, and Stephen J. Thoma, *Postconventional Moral Thinking: A Neo-Kohlbergian Approach* (Mahwah, N.J.: Lawrence Erlbaum, 1999).

7. David Moshman, "The Construction of Moral Rationality," *Human Development* 38 (1995): 275 (emphasis added).

8. In the fall of 1998, 73.9% of students in the Creighton University College of Arts & Sciences were of Caucasian background, while only 3.4% were Hispanic; for entering freshmen that same semester, 48% listed family incomes of $75,000 or more, while the income for 25% was more than $100,000; 35% of their mothers had a college degree, and 29% had a graduate degree or had done graduate work; for fathers, the figures were, respectively, 30% and 41%. This gives some idea of the backgrounds of the students of *Semestre Dominicano* 1998, and of the different context that they encountered in a developing country like the Dominican Republic. Thanks to Dr. Stephanie Wernig, Director of Institutional Research at Creighton, for this data.

9. Quoted anonymously with the permission of the student.

10. The principle texts for my Christology course were Brian McDermott, S.J., *Word Become Flesh: Dimensions of Christology* (Collegeville, Minn.: Liturgical Press, 1993) and Jon Sobrino, S.J., *Jesus in Latin America* (Maryknoll, N.Y.: Orbis Books, 1987), both of which could be used at the graduate level.

11. Kennedy, 249–55.

12. Robert A. Evans, "Education for Emancipation: Movement Toward Transformaton," in *Pedagogies for the Non-Poor*, 274.

13. Martin L. Hoffman, *Empathy and Moral Development: Implications for Caring and Justice* (Cambridge: Cambridge University Press, 2000), 30.

14. Jack Mezirow, *Transformative Dimensions of Adult Learning* (San Francisco: Jossey-Bass, 1991), 176.

15. Hoffman, 85.

16. Ibid., 182.

17. Ibid., 228–29; emphasis in original.

18. Ibid., 11–12; emphasis added.

19. Ibid., 107.

20. Ivan Illich, "To Hell with Good Intentions," in *Combining Service and Learning: A Resource Book for Community and Public Service*, ed. Jane C. Kendall and Associates, 314–20 (Raleigh, N.C.: National Society for Internships and Experiential Education, 1990).

21. Brueggemann, "Passion and Perspective," 72–73 (emphasis in original).

22. Hoffman, 13.

23. Ibid., 18–19.

24. Ibid., 185.

25. Mezirow, *Transformative Dimensions*, 168–69. For an application of Mezirow's theory to a program conducted by a U.S. community college in Nicaragua, see Richard Kiely, "A Transformational Learning Model for Service-Learning: A Longitudinal Case Study," *Michigan Journal of Community Service Learning* 12/1 (Fall 2005): 5–22. A companion piece, Kiely, "A Chameleon with a Complex: In Search of Transformation in International Service-Learning," *Michigan Journal of Community Service-Learning* 10/2 (Spring 2004); 5–20, is particularly revealing about the difficulty of reentry or reintegration into one's home culture, Mezirow's point #10, after such an experience.

26. Lynn Hunt, *Inventing Human Rights: A History* (New York: W.W. Norton, 2007), 33–34.

27. Adam Hochschild, *Bury the Chains: Prophets and Rebels in the Fight to Free an Empire's Slaves* (Boston: Houghton Mifflin, 2005), 366. And if these evangelical prophets placed less hope in the authority of the Bible than in human empathy, so much less should Catholic social activists today place hope in the authority of Catholic social teaching itself than in the experience of personal encounter with the poor.

28. Ibid., 3.

29. Ibid., 348.

30. Laurent A. Parks Daloz, Cheryl H. Keen, James P. Keen, and Sharon Daloz Parks, *Common Fire: Leading Lives of Commitment in a Complex World* (Boston: Beacon Press, 1996).

31. Ibid., 5.

32. Ibid., 63.

33. Sharon Daloz Parks, *Big Questions, Worthy Dreams: Mentoring Young Adults in Their Search for Meaning, Purpose, and Faith* (San Francisco: Jossey-Bass, 2000).

34. Ibid., 140.

35. Quoted in John Neafsey, *A Sacred Voice Is Calling: Personal Vocation and Social Conscience* (Maryknoll, N.Y.: Orbis Books, 2006), 164.

36. Walter Brueggemann, *The Prophetic Imagination* (Minneapolis: Fortress Press, 2001), 56.

5. "We Make the Road by Stumbling": Aristotle, Service-Learning, and Justice

1. Paulo Freire, *Pedagogy of Hope: Reliving Pedagogy of the Oppressed* (New York: Continuum, 1997), 24–26.

2. Jean Piaget, *The Moral Judgment of the Child* (New York: Free Press, 1932/1997).

3. Thanks to Jay W. Brandenberger for calling attention to this passage in *Pedagogy of Hope*, in his "Developmental Psychology and Service-learning: A Theoretical Framework," in *With Service in Mind: Concepts and Models for Service-learning in Psychology*, ed. Robert G. Bringle and Donna K. Duffy (Washington, D.C.: American Association for Higher Education, 1998), 68–84 (see 79).

4. "Ever since he wrote his thesis to become Professor of History and the Philosophy of Education at the University of Recife, Paulo Freire has referred to John Dewey, quoting his work *Democracy and Education*, published in Brazil in 1936." Moacir Gadotti, *Reading Paulo Freire: His Life and Work* (Albany: SUNY Press, 1994), 117.

5. "As a form of experiential education, service-learning has its roots in Dewey's theory of experience, which 'has become the touchstone of the experiential movement. . . .'" Barbara Jacoby & Associates, *Service-learning in Higher Education* (San Francisco: Jossey-Bass, 1996), 12. For a comparison of "the educational and philosophical theories of John Dewey and Paul Freire," see Thomas Deans, "Service-learning in Two Keys," *Michigan Journal of Community Service Learning*, 6 (Fall 1999): 15–29.

6. Kristján Kristjánsson, "The Do-Gooder, the Vain, the Generous, and Moral Education," *Education, Citizenship and Social Justice* 1/3 (2006): 280.

7. Roger Bergman, "Aristotle for Contemporary Moral Educators," *Journal of Research in Character Education* 5/1 (2007): 71–82.

8. *We Make the Road by Walking: Conversations on Education and Social Change: Myles Horton and Paulo Freire*, ed. Brenda Bell, John Gaventa, and John Peters (Philadelphia: Temple University Press, 1990). Myles Horton was the founder of the Highlander Folk School in Tennessee, where many leaders of the civil rights movement, including Rosa Parks, were trained. It was renamed The Highlander Research and Education Center.

9. Howard J. Curzer, "Aristotle's Painful Path to Virtue," *Journal of the History of Philosophy* 40/2 (2002): 141–62.

10. Joseph Kahne and Joel Westheimer, "Social Justice, Service Learning, and Higher Education: A Critical Review of Research," *The School Field* XII, 5/6 (2001): 31–42.

11. All page citations in this section are to Kristjánsson, "The Do-Gooder" (see note 6).

12. As will be indicated later in this chapter, Kristjánsson is aware that such philanthropy by itself might not be the best or even an adequate response to the global injustice of childhood mortality attributable to systemic poverty.

13. Kristjánsson, 280, quoting the character Clamence in Albert Camus' novel *The Fall*.

14. All page citations in sub-section "A shocking experience" are to Kerry Ann Rockquemore and Regan Harwell Schaeffer, "Toward a Theory of Engagement: A Cognitive Mapping of Service-learning Experiences," *Michigan Journal of Community Service Learning* 7 (Fall 2000): 14–25.

15. All page citations in sub-section "I feel the anger" are to Lee Artz, "Critical Ethnography for Communication Studies: Dialogue and Social Justice in Service-learning," *Southern Communication Journal* 66/3 (Spring 2001): 239–50.

16. All page citations in sub-section "Rattled to the bone" are to Michelle Dunlap, Jennifer Scoggin, Patrick Green, and Angelique Davi, "White Students' Experiences of Privilege and Socioeconomic Disparities: Toward a Theoretical Model," *Michigan Journal of Community Service Learning* 13/2 (Spring 2007): 19–30.

17. All page citations in sub-section "A bad feeling in my stomach" are to James M. Ostrow, "Self-Consciousness and Social Position: On College Students Changing Their Minds About Homelessness," *Qualitative Sociology* 18/3 (1995): 357–75.

18. All page citations in this section are to Curzer, "Aristotle's Painful Path."

19. Michael Schratz and Rob Walker, "Service-learning as Education: Learning from the Experience of Experience," in *Teaching for Justice: Concepts and Models for Service-learning in Peace Studies*, ed. Kathleen Maas Weigert and Robin J. Crews (Washington, D.C.: American Association for Higher Education, 1999).

20. Katherine Kirby, "Courageous Faith and Moral Formation: Trust, Respect, and Self-Confidence." Paper presented at the conference of the Association for Moral Education at the University of Notre Dame, November 13–15, 2008.

21. Kolvenbach, "The Service of Faith," 155.

6. Meetings with Remarkable Men and Women: On Teaching Moral Exemplars

1. Franz Jägerstätter in Gordon Zahn, *In Solitary Witness: The Life and Death of Franz Jägerstätter* (Springfield, Ill.: Templegate, 1986): 237.

2. All quotations from the *Rhetoric* will be from the W. Rhys Roberts translation in *The Complete Works of Aristotle: The Revised Oxford Translation, Volume Two*, ed. Jonathan Barnes (Princeton, N.J.: Princeton University Press, 1984).

3. John Coleman, "Conclusion: After Sainthood?" in *Saints and Virtues*, ed. John Stratton Hawley (Berkeley: University of California Press, 1987), 212.

4. Friedrich Nietzsche, *Schopenhauer as Educator* (Chicago: Henry Regnery Company, 1965).

5. Andrew Michael Flescher, *Heroes, Saints, and Ordinary Morality* (Washington, D.C.: Georgetown University Press, 2003).

6. Flescher, *Heroes*, 6 (emphasis in original).

7. MacIntyre, "Plain Persons," 146.

8. Michael Woods, trans., *Aristotle, Eudemian Ethics: Books I, II, and VIII*, Second edition (Oxford: Clarendon Press, 1992).

9. MacIntyre, *After Virtue*, 178.

10. David Ross, trans., *Aristotle: The Nicomachean Ethics* (Oxford, U.K.: Oxford Univesity Press, 1998). Translations in brackets are from Christopher Rowe, trans., *Aristotle Nicomachean Ethics* (Oxford: Oxford University Press, 2002).

11. John Rawls, *A Theory of Justice* (Cambridge, Mass.: Harvard University Press, 1971), 426.

12. Ibid., 427–28.

13. Ibid., 428 (emphasis added). Rawls's explication of the Aristotelian Principle was called to my attention by Flescher: 262–63. As the following discussion suggests, however, it would seem that Rawls's statement that we "enjoy" observing the abilities of others underplays the painful dimension of emulation.

14. Ibid., 427.

15. Anne Colby and William Damon, *Some Do Care: Contemporary Lives of Moral Commitment* (New York: Free Press, 1992): x.

16. Ibid., 29; see also their Appendix A: The Nominating Study.

17. For another contemporary list of "good things," see Flescher's criteria in *Heroes* (154) for moral heroism, which overlap partially with Colby's and Damon's criteria for moral exemplars.

18. Rebekah Nathan, *My Freshman Year: What a Professor Learned by Becoming a Student* (Ithaca, N.Y.: Cornell University Press, 2005). "Rebekah Nathan" is the pseudonym of Professor Cathy Small, who "became" a freshman at her own university in order to research student culture.

19. Ibid., 146–47.

20. Ibid., 147.

21. Ibid., 147.

22. Kristján Kristjánsson, "Emulation and the Use of Role Models in Moral Education," *Journal of Moral Education* 35/1 (2006): 45.

23. Ibid., 45 (emphasis in original).

24. Lawrence Cunningham, *The Meaning of Saints* (San Francisco: Harper and Row, 1980).

25. John Stratton Hawley, "Introduction: Saints and Virtues," in *Saints and Virtues*, ed. John Stratton Hawley (Berkeley: University of California Press, 1987), xiii.

26. Ibid., xvi.

27. Coleman, "After Sainthood?", 217.

28. Ibid., 218; quoting Paul Waddell.

29. Cunningham, *Meaning*, 83.

30. Ron Hansen, "The Pilgrim: Saint Ignatius of Loyola," in *An Ignatian Spirituality Reader*, ed. George W. Traub, S.J. (Chicago: Loyola Press, 2008): 28.

31. Flescher, *Heroes*, 7.

32. M. F. Burnyeat, "Aristotle on Learning to Be Good," in *Essays on Aristotle's Ethics*, ed. Amélie Oksenberg Rorty (Berkeley: University of California Press, 1980): 78.

33. Ibid., 79 (emphasis added).

34. Ibid., 69.

35. Kristjánsson, "Emulation," 45.

36. Quoted anonymously with permission of the student.

37. I suspect that it is not only young people who feel something like shame when comparing themselves with someone like Dr. King. Even relatively morally mature adults might feel something similar. I'll address this issue later in the chapter, with the help of Flescher's ideas on "the developmental imperative." See the "Personal Postscript" section of this chapter.

38. Quoted in Chmiel, *The Book of Mev*, 374. See Puleo, *The Struggle Is One*. Robert McAffee Brown in his Foreword identifies Mev's book as his choice "to introduce North Americans to the real meaning of liberation theology," ix.

39. Kristjánsson, "Emulation," 47.

40. Hartnett, "Heuristics," 71.

41. James Conant, "Nietzsche's Perfectionism: A Reading of *Schopenhauer as Educator*," in *Nietzsche's Postmoralism: Essays on Nietzsche's Prelude to Philosophy's Future*, ed. Richard Schachter (Cambridge: Cambridge University Press, 2001), 191. All page citations in this section will be to this article unless otherwise indicated.

42. Nietzsche, *Schopenhauer*, 5.

43. Flescher, *Heroes*, 4.

44. Tracy Kidder, *Mountains Beyond Mountains* (New York: Random House, 2003), 244.

45. Quoted anonymously with permission of the student.

46. Flescher, *Heroes*, 8.

47. Ibid., 279.

48. Ibid., 19.

49. Ibid., 241.

50. Ibid., 8.

51. Curzer, "Aristotle's Painful Path," 141–62.

52. Flescher, *Heroes*, 12.

53. From his "Prison Statement," Appendix I, in Gordan Zahn, *In Solitary Witness: The Life and Death of Franz Jägerstätter* (Springfield, Ill.: Templegate Publishers, 1986), 237.

54. Flescher, *Heroes*, 320.

55. Philip Hallie, *Lest Innocent Blood Be Shed: The Story of the Village of Le Chambon and How Goodness Happened There* (San Francisco: Harper and Row, 1979), 154.

56. Quoted anonymously with permission of the student.

57. "In Class with Romero" was originally published in *America*, May 11, 2009, and is reprinted with the permission of America Press, Inc., http://americamagazine.org.

58. *Gaudium et Spes*, #16.

7. Education for Justice and the Catholic University: Innovation or Development? An Argument from Tradition

A version of this chapter was accepted for publication in the *Journal of Catholic Higher Education* but had not yet appeared as this book went to press. The author would like to thank the editor for permission to use it here and to the editors and anonymous reviewers whose comments led to substantial improvements in the original manuscript.

1. David Hollenbach, S.J., "Comment," in *Catholic Universities in Church and Society: a Dialogue on Ex Corde Ecclesiae*, ed. John P. Langan, S.J. (Washington, D.C.: Georgetown University Press, 1993), 94.

2. Kolvenbach, "Service of Faith," 158–59.

3. Synod of Bishops, "Justice in the World," in O'Brien and Shannon, *Catholic Social Thought*, 289.

4. Pope John Paul II, "*Ex Corde Ecclesiae*: On Catholic Universities," in *Catholic Universities in Church and Society: A Dialogue on Ex Corde Ecclesiae*, ed. John P. Langan, S.J. (Washington, D.C.: Georgetown University Press, 1993), 231.

5. Charles J. Beirne, S.J., *Jesuit Education and Social Change in El Salvador* (New York: Garland, 1996), 228.

6. This tripartite understanding of the reach of justice within the university—formation and learning, teaching and research, and the institution's "way of proceeding"—was articulated by Fr. Kolvenbach, in his address at Santa Clara University in 2000.

7. In 1998, the Task Force on Catholic Social Teaching and Catholic Education of the U.S. Conference of Catholic Bishops reported "that while there is clear interest in and support for Catholic social teaching among [Catholic] institutions of higher education, it is generally not offered in a systematic way. . . . The task of convincing faculties that these are intellectually serious matters appears to be an important challenge." *Sharing Catholic Social Teaching: Challenges and Directions: Reflections of the U.S. Catholic Bishops*, (Washington, D.C.: Unites States Catholic Conference, 1998), 15–16.

8. John Henry Newman, *The Idea of a University* (Notre Dame, Ind.: University of Notre Dame Press, 1982), 10. Page citations in this section are to this volume unless otherwise indicated.

9. Pope Leo XIII, *Rerum Novarum*, in O'Brien and Shannon, *Catholic Social Thought*, 14–39.

10. Martin J. Svaglic, Introduction to Newman, *Idea*, xiii.

11. The title of a series of conferences of the 28 Jesuit colleges and universities, beginning at Santa Clara University in 2000, where Fr. Kolvenbach gave his famous address.

12. John W. O'Malley, S.J., "How the First Jesuits Became Involved in Education," in Duminuco, *Jesuit Ratio Studiorum*, 64.

13. William W. Meissner, S.J., *Ignatius of Loyola: The Psychology of a Saint* (New Haven: Yale, 1992), 15.

14. Ibid., 154. Iñigo took the name at about age 50 in homage to St. Ignatius of Antioch.

15. Robert R. Rusk, *The Doctrine of the Great Educators* (London: Macmillan, 1956), 86. Quoted in George Ganss, S.J., *Saint Ignatius' Idea of a Jesuit University* (Milwaukee: Marquette, 1956), 200, n. 25. Page citations in this section are to Ganss unless otherwise indicated.

16. O'Malley, "First Jesuits," 74.

17. Howard Gray, S.J., "Soul Education: An Ignatian Priority," in Traub, *Jesuit Education Reader*, 196. Gray reports that Ganss, in his translation of the *Constitutions* of the Society, "notes that *animas* in Ignatius' Spanish means 'the person,' first the men of the Society and their entire selves, and then the persons they serve—men and women in their total reality." Knowledge, for Ignatius, was for the sake of others as whole persons, as created and redeemed by God.

18. O'Malley, "First Jesuits," 58–59.

19. "Common good" here is no importation from the twentieth century. "When St. Ignatius spoke of schools, he in fact described them as a work of charity, a contribution to what he called the 'common good' of society at large." Ibid., 64.

20. Ibid., 59 (emphasis added).

21. Ibid., 59.

22. Michael J. Buckley, S.J., *The Catholic University as Promise and Project: Reflections in a Jesuit Idiom* (Washington, D.C.: Georgetown University Press, 1998), 92.

23. Ibid., 81.

24. O'Malley, "First Jesuits," 60.

25. Ibid., 61 (emphasis in original).

26. Ibid., 64.

27. Ibid., 66.

28. Ibid., 68.

29. Formation according to Matthew 25:36–41.

30. Modras, *Ignatian Humanism*, 51–84.

31. Ganss, *Ignatius' Idea*, x.

32. Ibid., 45.

33. O'Malley, "First Jesuits," 64.

34. Ibid., 59.

35. John Paul II, *Ex Corde Ecclesiae*, 229–53. All subsequent citations from *Ex Corde Ecclesiae* will be to paragraph numbers as given in this text.

36. Michael J. Buckley, S.J., "Education Marked with the Sign of the Cross," in Traub, *Jesuit Education Reader*, 139.

37. Ibid., 140.

38. Ibid., 142.

39. Ibid., 143.

40. Ignacio Ellacuría, "Is a Different Kind of University Possible?", in *Towards A Society That Serves Its People*, ed. John Hassett and Hugh Lacey (Washington, D.C.: Georgetown University Press, 1991), 198.

41. Ellacuría, "Different Kind," 198 (emphasis in original).

42. Kolvenbach, "The Service of Faith," 156.

43. Buckley, "Sign of the Cross," 143.

44. Other Catholic universities offer similar programs: e.g., Santa Clara University in El Salvador and Xavier University in Nicaragua. For a description of Santa Clara's Casa de la Solidaridad and of its students' experiences in the program, see Kevin Yonkers-Talz, "A Learning Partnership: U.S. College Students and the Poor in El Salvador," in *Learning Partnerships: Theory and Models of Practice to Educate for Self-Authorship*, ed. Marcia B. Baxter Magolda and Patricia M. King (Sterling, Va.: Stylus, 2004), 151–84.

8. Aristotle, Ignatius, and the Painful Path to Solidarity: A Pedagogy for Justice in Catholic Higher Education

1. Quoted in *Hearts on Fire: Praying with Jesuits*, ed. Michael Harter, S.J. (St. Louis: Institute of Jesuit Sources, 1993), 65.

2. See *Crossing Borders, Challenging Boundaries: A Guide to the Pedagogy and Philosophy of the Center for Global Education* (Minneapolis: Augusburg College, 1988) as well as Elisabeth Hayes and Sondra Cuban, "Border Pedagogy: A Critical Framework for Service-Learning," *Michigan Journal of Community Service Learning*, 4 (Fall 1997): 72–80.

3. Kerry Ann Rockquemore and Regan Harwell Schaeffer, "Toward a Theory of Engagement: A Cognitive Mapping of Service-learning Experiences," *Michigan Journal of Community Service Learning* 7 (Fall 2000): 16.

4. Dom Helder Camara, *The Desert Is Fertile* (Maryknoll, N.Y.: Orbis Books, 1982), p. 54.

5. James W. Fowler, *Stages of Faith: The Psychology of Human Development and the Quest for Meaning* (San Francisco: Harper & Row, 1981).

6. James W. Fowler, "Faith and the Fault Lines of Shame," Part II of *Faithful Change: The Personal and Public Challenges of Postmodern Life* (Nashville, Tenn.: Abingdon,

1996), 89–144. All page citations in the section "When shame is not a grace" are to this text.

7. "But at this time he had much to suffer from scruples. . . . although he knew these scruples were doing him much harm and that it would be good to be rid of them, he could not shake them off." Young, *St. Ignatius' Own Story*, #22.

8. For a brief but profound theological exploration of the similar phenomenon of "group cultural disparagement," see Thomas Clarke, S.J., "Option for the Poor: A Reflection," *America* (January 30, 1988), 95–99. This is the most insightful, compelling meditation on the "Social Gospel" I've ever read. It is, of course, quite possible for a child to develop healthy shame in a family of minority status. One thinks of Martin Luther King, Jr., although his family also held an honorable status within the black community itself. The contrast with the childhood of Malcolm X, whose family, even though living in the North, was repeatedly and consistently exposed to racist violence and oppression, could hardly be more striking. See James H. Cone, *Martin and Malcolm and America: A Dream or a Nightmare* (Maryknoll, N.Y.: Orbis Books, 1991).

9. Jeffrey D. Thielman and Raymond A. Schroth, S.J., *Volunteer with the Poor in Peru* (Bloomington, Ind.: 1st Books Library, 2000), 9–10.

10. For an iconic performance by Johnny Cash, see http://www.youtube.com/watch?v=hP67H4qfe5w.

11. For a "high" cultural meditation on a not dissimilar theme, see Wallace Stevens's great poem, "*Sunday Morning*," in *Poems by Wallace Stevens*, Selected and with an Introduction by Samuel French Morse (New York: Vintage, 1959), 7–10.

12. *Spiritual Exercises* #48 (emphasis added). The English translations of the *Exercises* are many and the accompanying secondary literature is vast. See for example, *The Spiritual Exercises of Saint Ignatius*, trans. and with commentary by Pierre Wolff (Ligouori, Mo.: Triumph, 1997).

13. Ignatius used the Spanish verb *sentir*, which suggests both feeling and understanding. See Dean Brackley, S.J., *The Call to Discernment in Troubled Times: New Perspectives on the Transformative Wisdom of Ignatius of Loyola* (New York: Crossroad, 2004), 21–24.

14. Walter Wink, *The Powers That Be: Theology for a New Millennium* (New York: Doubleday, 1998).

15. As of May, 2010, 63 students have completed the Justice and Peace Studies minor, and 30 have completed the more recent Justice and Society major.

16. *Encuentro Dominicano* is the successor to *Semestre Dominicano*, the subject of Chapter 4. *Semestre* ran from 1992 to 2003 when it was put on hiatus to be redesigned as *Encuentro*, which began in 2005. More than 300 students have participated in these programs.

17. Some students, developing a taste for this sort of education, do both the Dominican and Salvadoran programs.

18. For an excellent analysis of the role of practical reason in such a course, see Todd D. Whitmore, "Practicing the Common Good: The Pedagogical Implications of

Catholic Social Teaching," *Teaching Theology and Religion*, 3/1 (2000): 3–19. For discussion of a CST course incorporating service-learning, see Margaret R. Pfeil, "Experiential Learning in Service of a Living Tradition," in *Theology and The New Histories*, ed. Gary Macy (Maryknoll, N.Y.: Orbis Books, 1988): 245–60. Pfeil makes the following observation, which is also the fundamental theme of this book: "If our educational journey had been confined strictly to classroom learning, I am certain the bishops' call for economic justice [in their 1986 pastoral letter] would have been summarily dismissed as an unattainable utopian ideal. But, through the experiential learning component, students almost inevitably found themselves grappling with the implications of the bishops' call to embrace the option for the poor" (p. 252).

19. "In the twelfth century, when Peter Abelard wished to exercise the theological ingenuity of his students, he presented them with a series of conflicting 'authorities,' the famous *Sic et Non*. Included among the theses and antitheses was the proposition that 'Christians are not allowed for any reason to kill anyone, and the contrary [view].' Abelard knew, of course, that opinions could be adduced from Christian tradition to support both sides of the argument, and he set before his students the task, of resolving, if possible, the contradictions." David G. Hunter, "A Decade of Research on Early Christians and Military Service," *Religious Studies Review* 18/2 (1992): 87.

20. Patricia M. King and Karen Strohm Kitchener, *Developing Reflective Judgment* (San Francisco: Jossey-Bass, 1994).

21. In the most recent iteration of this course, six of the 17 guest speakers were JPS graduates.

22. Fr. Larry Gillick's, S.J., message in a nutshell: If you think God has a blueprint for your life, and all you have to do is find and follow it, you have just made God obsolete.

23. The two majors that have been the exceptions are, ironically, Social Work and Education because many students in those departments would be interested. But preprofessional requirements for those majors have been so heavy that there has been little room left in a student's schedule for a minor. Recent changes in the Social Work curriculum have made it possible for students to double-major in SW and Justice and Society.

24. All the student authors have given permission for these excerpts to be quoted anonymously. I have hoped thereby to mitigate any difficult feelings on the part of the many students who have written compellingly of their experiences but who are not quoted.

25. *Mohandas Gandhi: Essential Writings*, ed. John Dear, S.J. (Maryknoll, N.Y.: Orbis Books, 2002), 190–91.

26. Parks, *Big Questions*. In addition to this excellent book, other influences on the development of this concluding section include Colby and Damon, *Some Do Care* and Larry P. Nucci, *Education in the Moral Domain* (Cambridge, U.K.: Cambridge University Press, 2001).

REFERENCES

Anderson, E. Byron, and Bruce T. Morrill, eds. *Liturgy and the Moral Self: Humanity at Full Stretch Before God—Essays in Honor of Don E. Saliers.* Collegeville, Minn.: Liturgical Press, 1998.

Artz, Lee. "Critical Ethnography for Communication Studies: Dialogue and Social Justice in Service-Learning." *Southern Communication Journal* 66/3 (Spring 2001): 239–50.

Barnes, Jonathan, ed. *The Complete Works of Aristotle: The Revised Oxford Translation: Volume Two.* Princeton, N.J.: Princeton University Press, 1984.

Beirne, Charles J., S.J. *Jesuit Education and Social Change in El Salvador.* New York: Garland, 1996.

Bell, Brenda, John Gaventa, and John Peters, eds. *We Make the Road by Walking: Conversations on Education and Social Change: Myles Horton and Paulo Freire.* Philadelphia: Temple University Press, 1990.

Bennett, William J. *The Book of Virtues: A Treasury of Great Moral Stories.* New York: Simon & Schuster, 1993.

Bergman, Roger. "Aristotle for Contemporary Moral Educators." *Journal of Research in Character Education* 5/1 (2007): 71–82.

———. "The Bath" and "Sacrifice at the Dump." *Sojourners*, May, 1982: 17.

———. "Education for Justice and the Catholic University: Innovation or Development? An Argument from Tradition." Forthcoming in the *Journal of Catholic Higher Education.*

———. "In Class With Romero," *America*, May 11, 2009.
———. "Recent U.S. Perceptions of Haiti and Haitians." *Journal for Peace and Justice Studies* 5/2 (1993): 133–44.
———. "Sumpul, River of Infants." *Studia Mystica* V/4 (1982): 48.
———. "Teaching Justice After MacIntyre: Toward a Catholic Philosophy of Moral Education." *Catholic Education: A Journal of Inquiry and Practice* 12/1 (2008): 7–24.
Brackley, Dean, S.J. *The Call to Discernment in Troubled Times: New Perspectives on the Transformative Wisdom of Ignatius of Loyola*. New York: Crossroad, 2004.
———. "The Christian University and Liberation: The Challenge of the UCA." *Discovery: Jesuit International Ministries* 2 (December 1992).
———. *Select Bibliography and Visual Resources (in English): El Salvador and Central America*. (The Church of the Poor, Archbishop Romero, the UCA Martyrs, the Four Churchwomen). http://www.sju.edu/libraries/drexel/special/elsalvador/el_salvador.htm.
Brandenberger, Jay W. "Developmental Psychology and Service-Learning: A Theoretical Framework." In *With Service in Mind: Concepts and Models for Service-Learning in Psychology*, edited by Robert G. Bringle and Donna K. Duffy, 68–84. Washington, D.C.: American Association for Higher Education, 1998.
Brockman, James R. *Romero: A Life*. Maryknoll, N.Y.: Orbis Books, 2005.
Brueggemann, Walter. "Passion and Perspective: Two Dimensions of Education in the Bible." In *Theological Perspectives on Christian Formation: A Reader on Theology and Christian Education*, edited by Jeff Astley, Leslie J. Francis, and Colin Crowder, 71–79. Grand Rapids, Mich.: Eerdmans, 1996.
———. [1978]. *The Prophetic Imagination*. Second edition. Minneapolis: Fortress Press, 2001.
Buckley, Michael J., S.J. *The Catholic University as Promise and Project: Reflections in a Jesuit Idiom*. Washington, D.C.: Georgetown University Press, 1998.
———. "Education Marked with the Sign of the Cross." In *A Jesuit Education Reader*, edited by George W. Traub, S.J., 138–43. Chicago: Loyola Press, 2008.

Burke, Kevin, S.J., ed. *Pedro Arrupe: Essential Writings*. Maryknoll, N.Y.: Orbis Books, 2004.

Burnyeat, M.F. "Aristotle on Learning to Be Good." In *Essays on Aristotle's Ethics*, edited by Amélie Oksenberg Rorty, 69–92. Berkeley: University of California Press, 1980.

Byron, William J., S.J. "Ten Building Blocks of Catholic Social Teaching." *America*, Oct. 31, 1998.

Camara, Dom Helder. *The Desert Is Fertile*. Maryknoll, N.Y.: Orbis Books, 1982.

Carrigan, Ana. *Roses in December: The Story of Jean Donovan* [film]. New York: First-Run Features, 1982.

Center for Global Education. *Crossing Borders, Challenging Boundaries: A Guide to the Pedagogy and Philosophy of the Center for Global Education*. Minneapolis: Augusburg College, 1988.

Chmiel, Mark. *The Book of Mev*. Bloomington, Ind.: Xlibris, 2005.

Clarke, Thomas, S.J. "Option for the Poor: A Reflection." *America*, January 30, 1988.

Colby, Anne and William Damon. *Some Do Care: Contemporary Lives of Moral Commitment*. New York: Free Press, 1992.

Conant, James. "Nietzsche's Perfectionism: A Reading of *Schopenhauer as Educator*." In *Nietzsche's Postmoralism: Essays on Nietzsche's Prelude to Philosophy's Future*, edited by Richard Schachter, 181–257. Cambridge: Cambridge University Press, 2001.

Cunningham, Lawrence. *The Meaning of Saints*. San Francisco: Harper & Row, 1980.

Curzer, Howard. "Aristotle's Painful Path to Virtue." *Journal of the History of Philosophy* 40/2 (2002): 141–62.

Daloz, Laurent A. Parks, Cheryl H. Keen, James P. Keen, and Sharon Daloz Parks. *Common Fire: Leading Lives of Commitment in a Complex World*. Boston: Beacon Press, 1996.

Deans, Thomas. "Service-learning in Two Keys." *Michigan Journal of Community Service Learning* 6 (1999): 15–29.

Dear, John, S.J., ed. *Mohandas Gandhi: Essential Writings*. Maryknoll, N.Y.: Orbis Books, 2002.

Duminuco, Vincent J., S.J., ed. *The Jesuit* Ratio Studiorum: *400th Anniversary Perspectives*. New York: Fordham University Press, 2000.

Dunlap, Michelle, Jennifer Scoggin, Patrick Green, and Anglelique Davi. "White Students' Experiences of Privilege and Socioeconomic Disparities: Toward a Theoretical Model." *Michigan Journal of Community Service Learning* 13/2 (Spring 2007): 19–30.

Dwyer, Judith A., ed. *The New Dictionary of Catholic Social Thought*. Collegeville, Minn.: Michael Glazier, 1994.

Ellacuría, Ignacio, S.J. "Is a Different Kind of University Possible?" In *Towards A Society That Serves Its People*, edited by John Hassett and Hugh Lacey, 177–207. Washington, D.C.: Georgetown University Press, 1991.

Ellsberg, Robert. *All Saints: Daily Reflections on Saints, Prophets, and Witnesses for Our Time*. New York: Crossroad, 1997.

Evans, Alice Frazer, Robert A. Evans, and William Bean Kennedy, eds. *Pedagogies for the Non-Poor*. Maryknoll, N.Y.: Orbis Books, 1987.

Flescher, Andrew Michael. *Heroes, Saints, and Ordinary Morality*. Washington, D.C.: Georgetown University Press, 2003.

Fogelman, Eva. *Conscience and Courage: Rescuers of Jews During the Holocaust*. New York: Anchor Books, 1994.

Forché, Carolyn. *The Country Between Us*. New York: Harper & Row, 1981.

Fowler, James W. *Faithful Change: The Personal and Public Challenges of Postmodern Life*. Nashville: Abingdon, 1996.

———. *Stages of Faith: The Psychology of Human Development and the Quest for Meaning*. San Francisco: Harper & Row, 1981.

Freire, Paulo. *Pedagogy of Hope: Reliving Pedagogy of the Oppressed*. Translated by Robert R. Barr. New York: Continuum, 1997.

———. *Pedadogy of the Oppressed*. Revised edition. Translated by Myra Bergman Ramos. New York: Continuum, 1994.

Fuller, Michael. *Making Sense of MacIntyre*. Aldershot, U.K.: Ashgate, 1998.

Gadotti, Moacir. *Reading Paulo Freire: His Life and Work*. Translated by John Milton. Albany: SUNY Press, 1994.

Ganss, George, S.J. *Saint Ignatius' Idea of a Jesuit University*. Milwaukee: Marquette University Press, 1956.

Giles, Jr., Dwight E. and Janet Eyler, "The Theoretical Roots of Service-Learning in John Dewey." *Michigan Journal of Community Service-Learning*, 1/1 (Fall 1994): 77–85.

Gray, Howard, S.J., "Soul Education: An Ignatian Priority." In *A Jesuit Education Reader*, edited by George Traub, S.J., 195–208. Chicago: Loyola Press, 2008.

Gutiérrez, Gustavo. *A Theology of Liberation: History, Politics, and Salvation*. Revised edition. Translated by Sr. Caridad Inda and John Eagleson. Maryknoll, N.Y.: Orbis Books, 1988.

Hallie, Philip. *Lest Innocent Blood Be Shed: The Story of the Village of Le Chambon and How Goodness Happened There*. New York: Harper & Row, 1979.

Hansen, Ron. "The Pilgrim: Saint Ignatius of Loyola." In *An Ignatian Spirituality Reader*, edited by George W. Traub, S.J., 24–44. Chicago: Loyola Press, 2008.

Hartnett, Dan, S.J. "The Heuristics of Justice." *Proceedings of the 65th Annual Meeting of the Jesuit Philosophical Association* (2004), 55–73.

Haughey, John C., S.J., ed. *The Faith That Does Justice: Examining the Christian Sources for Social Change*. New York: Paulist Press, 1977.

Hayes, Elisabeth and Sondra Cuban. "Border Pedagogy: A Critical Framework for Service-Learning." *Michigan Journal of Community Service Learning* 4 (Fall 1997): 72–80.

Hellwig, Monika. *The Eucharist and the Hunger of the World*. Second edition. Lanham, Md.: Sheed and Ward, 1992.

———. "Good News to the Poor: Do They Understand It Better?" In *Tracing the Spirit: Communities, Social Action, and Theological Reflection*," edited by James E. Hug, S.J., 122–48. Ramsey, N.J.: Paulist Press, 1983.

Himes, Kenneth R., O.F.M. *Responses to 101 Questions on Catholic Social Teaching*. Mahwah, N.J.: Paulist Press, 2001.

Himes, Kenneth R., O.F.M., ed. *Modern Catholic Social Teaching: Commentaries and Interpretations*. Washington, D.C.: Georgetown University Press, 2005.

Hochschild, Adam. *Bury the Chains: Prophets and Rebels in the Fight to Free an Empire's Slaves*. Boston: Houghton Mifflin, 2005.

Hoffman, Martin L. *Empathy and Moral Development: Implications for Caring and Justice*. Cambridge: Cambridge University Press, 2000.

Holland, Joe and Peter Henriot, S.J. *Social Analysis: Linking Faith and Justice*. Revised and enlarged edition. Maryknoll, N.Y.: Orbis Books, 1983.

Hollenbach, David, S.J. "A communitarian reconstruction of human rights: contributions from Catholic tradition." In *Catholicism and Liberalism: Contributions to American Public Philosophy*, edited by R. Bruce Douglass and David Hollenbach, 127–50. Cambridge: Cambridge University Press, 1994.

———. "Comment." In *Catholic Universities in Church and Society: A Dialogue on Ex Corde Esslesiae*, edited by John P. Langan, S.J., 90–94. Washington, D.C.: Georgetown University Press, 1993. John Horton and Susan Mendus, eds. *After MacIntyre: Critical Perspectives on the Work of Alasdair MacIntyre*. Notre Dame, Ind.: University of Notre Dame Press, 1994.

Hughes, Kathleen and Mark Francis, eds. *Living No Longer for Ourselves: Liturgy and Justice in the Nineties*. Collegeville, Minn.: Liturgical Press, 1991.

Hunt, Lynn. *Inventing Human Rights: A History*. New York: W.W. Norton, 2007.

Hunter, David G. "A Decade of Research on Early Christians and Military Service." *Religious Studies Review* 18/2 (1992): 87–94.

Illich, Ivan. "To Hell with Good Intentions." In *Combining Service and Learning: A Resource Book for Community and Public Service*, edited by Jane C. Kendall and Associates, 314–20. Raleigh, N.C.: National Society for Internships and Experiential Education, 1990.

Irwin, Terence, trans. *Aristotle. Nicomachean Ethics*. Second edition. Indianapolis: Hackett Publishing Company, 1999.

Jacoby, Barbara & Associates. *Service-Learning in Higher Education*. San Francisco: Jossey-Bass, 1996.

John Paul II. *Apostolic Constitution, Ex Corde Ecclesiae, of the Supreme Pontiff, John Paul II, on Catholic Universities*. In *Catholic Universities in Church and Society: A Dialogue on Ex Corde Ecclesiae*, edited by John P. Langan, S.J., 229–53. Washington, D.C.: Georgetown University Press, 1993.

Kahne, Joseph and Joel Westheimer. "Social Justice, Service Learning, and Higher Education: A Critical Review of Research." *The School Field* XII, 5/6 (2001): 31–42.

Kavanaugh, John F., S.J., and Mev Puleo. *Faces of Poverty, Faces of Christ*. Maryknoll, N.Y.: Orbis Books, 1991.

Kidder, Tracy. *Mountains Beyond Mountains*. New York: Random House, 2003.

Kiely, Richard. "A Chameleon with a Complex: Searching for Transformation in International Service-Learning." *Michigan Journal of Community Service Learning* 10/2 (Spring 2004): 5–20.

———. "A Transformational Learning Model for Service-Learning: A Longitudinal Case Study." *Michigan Journal of Community Service Learning* 12/1 (Fall 2005): 5–22.

King, Patricia M. and Karen Strohm Kitchener. *Developing Reflective Judgment*. San Francisco: Jossey-Bass, 1994.

Kirby, Katherine. "Courageous Faith and Moral Formation: Trust, Respect, and Self-Confidence." Paper presented at the conference of the Association for Moral Education at the University of Notre Dame, November 13–15, 2008. See her "Encountering and Understanding Suffering: The Need for Service Learning in Ethical Education," *Teaching Philosophy* 32/2 (June 2009): 153–76.

Knight, Kelvin. "Revolutionary Aristotelianism." *Contemporary Political Studies* 2 (1996): 885–96.

Knight, Kelvin, ed. *The MacIntyre Reader*. Notre Dame, Ind.: University of Notre Dame Press, 1998.

Kohlberg, Lawrence. "Education for Justice: A Modern Statement of the Platonic View." In *Moral Education: Five Lectures*, edited by Nancy F. and Theodore R. Sizer, 57–83. Cambridge, Mass.: Harvard University Press, 1970.

———. *Essays on Moral Development. Volume I: The Philosophy of Moral Development*. San Francisco: Harper and Row, 1981.

———. *Essays on Moral Development. Volume II: The Psychology of Moral Development*. San Francisco: Harper and Row, 1984.

Kolvenbach, Peter-Hans, S.J. "The Service of Faith and the Promotion of Justice in American Jesuit Higher Education." Address given at Santa Clara University, October 6, 2000. In *A Jesuit Education Reader*, edited by George W. Traub, S.J. (Chicago: Loyola Press, 1998): 144–62. http://onlineministries.creighton.edu/CollaborativeMinistry/kolvenbach_speech.html.

Kristjánsson, Kristján. "The Do-Gooder, the Vain, the Generous, and Moral Education." *Education, Citizenship and Social Justice* 1/3 (2006): 267–82.

———. "Emulation and the Use of Role Models in Moral Education." *Journal of Moral Education* 35/1 (2006): 37–49.

Langan, John, S.J., ed. *Catholic Universities in Church and Society: A Dialogue on Ex Corde Esslesiae.* Washington, D.C.: Georgetown University Press, 1993.

Lange, Martin and Reinhold Iblacker, S.J., eds. *Witnesses of Hope: The Persecution of Christians in Latin America.* Maryknoll, N.Y.: Orbis Books, 1981.

Lernoux, Penny. *Cry of the People: United States Involvement in the Rise of Fascism, Torture, and Murder and the Persecution of the Catholic Church in Latin America.* New York: Doubleday, 1980.

Lickona, Thomas. *Educating for Character: How Our Schools Can Teach Respect and Responsibility.* New York: Bantam, 1991.

Linscott, Mary, S.N.D. *Education and Justice.* Vatican City: The Pontifical Commission Justice and Peace, 1973.

MacIntyre, Alasdair. *After Virtue: A Study in Moral Theory.* Second edition. Notre Dame, Ind.: University of Notre Dame Press, 1984.

———. "Aquinas's Critique of Education: Against His Own Age, Against Ours." In *Philosophers on Education: New Historical Perspectives*, edited by Amélie Oksenberg Rorty, 95–108. London: Routledge, 1998.

———. "How to Seem Virtuous without Actually Being So." In *Education in Morality*, edited by J. Mark Halstead and Terence H. McLaughlin, 118–31. London: Routledge, 1999.

———. *Marxism and Christianity.* Second edition. London: Duckworth, 1995.

———. "Plain Persons and Moral Philosophers: Rules, Virtues, and Goods." In *The MacIntyre Reader*, edited by Kelvin Knight, 136–52. Notre Dame, Ind.: University of Notre Dame Press, 1998. Article originally published in 1992.

———. *Three Rival Versions of Moral Inquiry: Encyclopedia, Genealogy, and Tradition.* Gifford Lectures, University of Edinburgh, 1988. Notre Dame, Ind.: University of Notre Dame Press, 1990.

———. *Whose Justice? Which Rationality?* Notre Dame, Ind.: University of Notre Dame Press, 1988.

Maguire, Daniel. "The Feminist Turn in Social Ethics." In *Mainstreaming Feminist Research for Teaching Religious Studies*, edited by Arlene Swidler and Walter E. Conn, 77–83. Lanham, Md.: University Press of America, 1985.

Massaro, Thomas, S.J. *Living Justice: Catholic Social Teaching in Action*. Franklin, Wis.: Sheed and Ward, 2000. A revised Classroom Edition was published in 2008 by Rowman and Littlefield.

McKenna, Megan. *Rites of Justice: The Sacraments and Liturgy as Ethical Imperatives*. Maryknoll, N.Y.: Orbis Books, 1997.

Meissner, William W., S.J. *Ignatius of Loyola: The Psychology of a Saint*. New Haven: Yale, 1992.

Mezirow, Jack. *Transformative Dimensions of Adult Learning*. San Francisco: Jossey-Bass, 1991.

Mich, Marvin L. *Catholic Social Teaching and Movements*. Mystic, Conn.: Twenty-Third Publications, 1998.

Modras, Ronald. *Ignatian Humanism: A Dynamic Spirituality for the 21st Century*. Chicago: Loyola Press, 2004.

Monzu, Steven. *Student Leaders' Manual for the 2006 Freshmen Retreat*. Omaha, Neb.: Creighton Preparatory High School, 2006. My thanks to Steve Monzu, Director of Campus Ministry, for providing this resource.

Moshman, David. "The Construction of Moral Rationality." *Human Development* 38 (1995): 265–81.

Murphy, Madonna M. *Character Education in America's Blue Ribbon Schools: Best Practices for Meeting the Challenges*. Second edition. Lanham, Md.: Scarecrow Press, 2002.

Nathan, Rebekah. *My Freshman Year: What a Professor Learned by Becoming a Student*. New York: Penguin Books, 2005.

National Conference of Catholic Bishops. *Brothers and Sisters to Us: U.S. Bishops' Pastoral Letter on Racism in Our Day*. Washington, D.C.: National Conference of Catholic Bishops, 1979.

Neafsey, John. *A Sacred Voice Is Calling: Personal Vocation and Social Conscience*. Maryknoll, N.Y.: Orbis Books, 2006.

Newman, John Henry. *The Idea of a University*. Notre Dame, Ind.: University of Notre Dame Press, 1982.

Nietzsche, Friedrich. *Schopenhauer as Educator.* Translated by James W. Hillesheim and Malcolm R. Simpson. Chicago: Henry Regnery Company, 1965.

Nucci, Larry P. *Education in the Moral Domain.* Cambridge: Cambridge University Press, 2001.

O'Brien, David J., and Thomas A. Shannon, eds. *Catholic Social Thought: The Documentary Heritage.* Maryknoll, N.Y.: Orbis Books, 1992.

O'Hare, Padraic, ed. *Education for Peace and Justice.* San Francisco: Harper and Row, 1983.

Ostrow, James M. "Self-Consciousness and Social Position: On College Students Changing Their Minds About Homelessness." *Qualitative Sociology* 18/3 (1995): 357–75.

Parks, Sharon Daloz. *Big Questions, Worthy Dreams: Mentoring Young Adults in Their Search for Meaning, Purpose, and Faith.* San Francisco: Jossey-Bass, 2000.

Pfeil, Margaret R. "Experiential Learning in Service of a Living Tradition." In *Theology and The New Histories*, edited by Gary Macy, 245–60. Maryknoll, N.Y.: Orbis Books, 1988.

Piaget, Jean. [1932]. *The Moral Judgment of the Child.* Translated by Marjorie Gabain. New York: Free Press, 1997.

Pontifical Commission Justice and Peace. *The Church and Racism: Towards a More Fraternal Society.* Boston: St. Paul Books and Media, 1988. Republished in 2001 with "An Introductory Update" as a Contribution to the World Conference against Racism, Racial Discrimination, Xenophobia and Related Intolerance. http://www.ewtn.com/library/curia/pcjpchra.htm.

Power, Clark, Ann Higgins, and Lawrence Kohlberg. "The Habit of the Common Life: Building Character Through Democratic Community Schools." In *Moral Development and Character Education: A Dialogue*, edited by Larry Nucci, 125–43. Berkeley: McCutchan, 1989

Puleo, Mev. *The Struggle Is One: Voices and Visions of Liberation.* Albany: SUNY Press, 1994.

Rawls, John. *A Theory of Justice.* Cambridge, Mass.: Harvard University Press, 1971.

Rest, James, Darcia Narvaez, Muriel J. Bebeau, and Stephen J. Thoma. *Postconventional Moral Thinking: A Neo-Kohlbergian Approach.* Mahwah, N.J.: Lawrence Erlbaum, 1999.

Rockquemore, Kerry Ann, and Regan Harwell Schaeffer. "Toward a Theory of Engagement: A Cognitive Mapping of Service-learning Experiences." *Michigan Journal of Community Service Learning* 7 (Fall 2000): 14–5.

Ross, David, trans. *Aristotle. The Nicomachean Ethics*. Revised by J.L. Ackrill and J.O. Urmson. Oxford: Oxford University Press, 1998.

Rowe, Christopher, trans. *Aristotle. Nicomachean Ethics*. Oxford: Oxford University Press, 2002.

Ryan, Kevin, and Karen E. Bohlin. *Building Character in Schools: Practical Ways to Bring Moral Instruction to Life*. San Francisco: Jossey-Bass, 1999.

Schratz, Michael and Rob Walker. "Service-learning as Education: Learning from the Experience of Experience." In *Teaching for Justice: Concepts and Models for Service-learning in Peace Studies*, edited by Kathleen Maas Weigert and Robin J. Crews, 33–46. Washington, D.C.: American Association for Higher Education, 1999.

Searle, Mark, ed. *Liturgy and Social Justice*. Collegeville. Minn.: The Liturgical Press, 1980.

Segundo, Juan Luis, S.J. *The Liberation of Theology*. Maryknoll, N.Y.: Orbis Books, 1976.

Sobrino, Jon, S.J. *Christology at the Crossroads*. Maryknoll, N.Y.: Orbis Books, 1978.

Sobrino, Jon, S.J., Ignacio Ellacuría, S.J., and others. *Companions of Jesus: The Jesuit Martyrs of El Salvador*. Maryknoll, N.Y.: Orbis Books, 1990.

Spohn, William C. "The University That Does Justice." *Conversations on Jesuit Higher Education*, Spring, 2001.

Thielman, Jeffrey D. and Raymond A. Schroth, S.J. *Volunteer With the Poor in Peru*. Bloomington, Ind.: 1st Books Library, 2000. First published by Paulist Press in 1991.

Traub, George, S.J., ed. *A Jesuit Education Reader*. Chicago: Loyola Press, 2008.

United States Catholic Conference. *Sharing Catholic Social Teaching: Challenges and Directions: Reflections of the U.S. Catholic Bishops*. Washington, D.C.: United States Catholic Conference, 1998.

United States Conference of Catholic Bishops. *Forming Consciences for Faithful Citizenship: A Call to Political Responsibility from the Catholic*

Bishops of the United States. Washington, D.C.: United States Conference of Catholic Bishops, 2007.

Weigert, Kathleen Maas and Alexia K. Kelley, eds. *Living the Catholic Social Tradition: Cases and Commentary*. Lanham, Md.: Rowman and Littlefield, 2005.

Whitmore, Todd D. "Practicing the Common Good: The Pedagogical Implications of Catholic Social Teaching." *Teaching Theology and Religion* 3/1 (2000): 3–19.

Wijsen, Frans, Peter Henriot, and Rodrigo Mejia, eds. *The Pastoral Circle Revisted: A Critical Quest for Truth and Transformation*. Maryknoll, N.Y.: Orbis Books, 2005.

Wolff, Pierre, trans. *The Spiritual Exercises of Saint Ignatius*. Liguori, Mo.: Triumph, 1997.

Woods, Michael, trans. *Aristotle. Eudemian Ethics: Books I, II, and VIII*. Second edition. Oxford: Clarendon Press, 1992.

Yonkers-Talz, Kevin. "A Learning Partnership: U.S. College Students and the Poor in El Salvador." In *Learning Partnerships: Theory and Models of Practice to Educate for Self-Authorship*, edited by Marcia B. Baxter Magolda and Patricia M. King, 151–84. Sterling, Va.: Stylus, 2004.

Young, William J., trans. *St. Ignatius' Own Story As Told to Luis Gonzalez de Camara*. Chicago: Loyola University Press, 1998.

Zahn, Gordan. *In Solitary Witness: The Life and Death of Franz Jägerstätter*. Springfield, Ill.: Templegate Publishers, 1986.

INDEX